'This exceptional book is like th  *moriendi* model, shining light o has been in the shadows for to gentle and wise considerations tl the many faces and meanings of death.'
  – *Professor Rod MacLeod MNZM, Conjoint Professor in Palliative Care, University of Sydney, Australia*

'Dr Leget skillfully integrates his well-honed clinical sense with his in-depth understanding of some of the great thinkers of history to craft an approach to dying – and living – which respects both the uniqueness of each person and the wisdom of the ages. Bravo!'
  – *Rev George Handzo, HealthCare Chaplaincy Network, USA*

'There are many books on the market today which address issues of death and dying in society. This new book by Carlo Leget is more than just another addition to that literature. Expertly grounded in an academic theological and philosophical discourse, Professor Leget guides the reader through a contemporary reading of the medieval *Ars moriendi*, blending the wisdom of the past with a real-world understanding of the present. As a palliative care academic and practitioner, the crafting of this book, using evidence from the clinical setting, offers a reflection for the clinician and student on the complex dimensions of living and dying that they face on a daily basis. The "inner space" conceptual framework speaks to a yearning in our world today. This book helps to imagine how we might find it.'
  – *Philip Larkin, Professor of Clinical Nursing (Palliative Care), University College Dublin and Our Lady's Hospice and Care Services, Dublin, Ireland*

'Spiritual and existential issues are highly prevalent in patients with serious and/or life-threatening illnesses. All members of the care team need to be able to address these issues in a way that is compassionate but also clinically relevant. Leget's *Art of Living, Art of Dying* offers a simple framework for interpreting spiritual and existential questions with patients and helping them to cope with their suffering.

Building on the medieval *Ars moriendi* tradition, the author introduces a contemporary art of dying model, which demonstrates through case-based examples how members of the care team can discuss existential and spiritual questions in a respectful and non-judgemental way and in the context of a patient's health and wellbeing. I recommend this book not only for chaplains and clergy, but also for others on the healthcare team, including counsellors, doctors, nurses, allied healthcare workers and other professionals who come into contact with patients in hospitals and hospices.'

– Christina Puchalski, MD, FACP, FAAHPM,
Professor of Medicine, Director of the George
Washington Institute for Spirituality and Health,
George Washington University School of
Medicine and Health Sciences, USA

Art of Living, Art of Dying

Art of Living, Art of Dying

SPIRITUAL CARE FOR A GOOD DEATH

Carlo Leget

FOREWORD BY GEORGE FITCHETT

Jessica Kingsley *Publishers*
London and Philadelphia

First published in 2017
by Jessica Kingsley Publishers
73 Collier Street
London N1 9BE, UK
and
400 Market Street, Suite 400
Philadelphia, PA 19106, USA

www.jkp.com

Library of Congress Cataloging in Publication Data
Title: Art of living, art of dying : spiritual care for a good death / Carlo
  Leget ; foreword by George Fitchett.
Description: London ; Philadelphia : Jessica Kingsley Publishers, [2017] |
  Includes bibliographical references and index.
Identifiers: LCCN 2016044358 | ISBN 9781785922114 (alk. paper)
Subjects: LCSH: Death--Religious aspects. | Terminal care--Religious aspects.
Classification: LCC BL325.D35 L44 2017 | DDC 201/.762175--dc23 LC record
available at https://lccn.loc.gov/2016044358

British Library Cataloguing in Publication Data
A CIP catalogue record for this book is available from the British Library

ISBN 978 1 78592 211 4
eISBN 978 1 78450 491 5

Printed and bound in Great Britain

Dedicated to the loving memory of my sister
Angélique (1 November 1965 – 11 August 2016)

Contents

Foreword

It a pleasure to have Carlo Leget's description of his new *ars moriendi* model available in his book, *Art of Living, Art of Dying*. A brief description of the model has been available in English (Leget 2007), but now we have this thorough and well-written description of the model. This description includes case vignettes that illustrate the five themes in the model, elaboration of the dialectics that shape each theme, and insightful descriptions of current cultural influences on those dialectics.

A key metaphor in Leget's model is inner space. As he explains it, the metaphor has multiple meanings; one of them refers to the way our mind can be opened up when we feel heard and understood by another. I think three groups of readers will experience greater inner space regarding their thoughts and emotions about dying as they follow Leget's description of the *ars moriendi* model. First, when people are faced with serious or life threatening illness they and their loved ones may be overwhelmed with questions and emotions, with a polyphony of voices to use Leget's term. The five themes in his *ars moriendi* model may help them sort through those voices and begin to hear them differently. Support for this is suggested in Leget's description of a palliative care program in the Netherlands where patients are given a brochure with a brief description of the model and an invitation to talk with the palliative care nurse about thoughts and feelings evoked by reviewing it (see Chapter 10). Second, physicians, nurses, and other health professionals who work in palliative care or other end of life contexts have undoubtedly met some people who face death with great peace and others who suffer intensely. These encounters may raise what Leget calls "big questions" about the end of life for these health professionals. Becoming familiar with his new *ars moriendi* model may help open inner space for them to engage these questions, to deepen their understanding of such people and to help them provide more effective care for them.

Those who provide spiritual care for people who are at the end of life are the third group of readers who will find Leget's model helps them develop greater inner space. As someone who teaches spiritual care providers, chaplains, in the US context I wish to expand on this. In the US, chaplains are challenged by the growing secularization of the US population, including the growth of those who identify as spiritual but not religious. Chaplains who work in end of life care need a model that helps them understand and work with the spiritual needs of this group. The five themes in Leget's new *ars moriendi* are described in a broad non-parochial language that will be very relevant for this population. At the same time, Leget argues that themes in the model can be elaborated in the context of specific faith traditions and he shows what that looks like for Catholicism. This suggests the value of the model when chaplains are working with believers from diverse faith traditions.

A second challenge for chaplains in the US and elsewhere is the need to describe the benefits associated with their care. This has been described as outcome-oriented chaplaincy

(Handzo *et al.* 2014). The way chaplains are trained in the US causes some to resist this approach and leaves even those who affirm it poorly equipped to implement it. The main reason for this is the strong emphasis in our training on self-awareness and interpersonal communication skills and the limited emphasis on other important areas such as needs assessment and interventions. As Leget notes in the final chapter, familiarity with the *ars moriendi* model will enable chaplains working with people at the end of life to be attuned to themes they might tend to overlook and to document areas of spiritual need related to the themes in ways that other members of the health care team can learn to recognize and appreciate. Most importantly, because the five themes in the model can inform a description of spiritual needs they also support the description of changes in those needs associated with the chaplains' spiritual care; that is, the documentation of the effects of the chaplains' care on identifiable outcomes.

The emphasis in their training on developing self-awareness will cause chaplains to respond very positively to Leget's descriptions of the need for caregivers to cultivate their own inner space. But chaplains are frequently unable to see the larger connections between self-awareness, 'being present', and outcomes (Lyndes *et al.* 2012). Leget's work will help chaplains see those connections; specifically the links between their self-awareness (inner space) and their ability to foster inner space that will help patients (and/or their families) resolve tensions related to the five themes in the *ars moriendi* model. That is, it will help chaplains make the link between personal preparation, the process of care, and the outcomes that may occur because of that care.

Developing an evidence-based approach to care is an important challenge for healthcare chaplains. Can this book about *ars moriendi*, the art of dying, contribute to an effort to advance spiritual care research in the end of life context? I think it can. Research can test whether the five themes in the model encompass the central spiritual concerns expressed by patients who are confronting their death. Research can also examine the kinds of interventions that are most effective in opening the inner space that helps patients wrestling with those themes. Patients, their families, health professionals, and especially chaplains, will receive a great deal from careful study of this thoughtful and important book.

George Fitchett

References

Handzo, G.F., Cobb, M., Holmes, C., Kelly, E. and Sinclair, S. (2014) 'Outcomes for professional health care chaplaincy: an international call to action.' *Journal of Health Care Chaplaincy, 20*, 2, 43–53.

Leget, C. (2007) 'Retrieving the ars moriendi tradition.' Medicine, *Health Care and Philosophy, 10*, 3, 313–9.

Lyndes, K. A., Fitchett, G., Berlinger, N., Cadge, W., Misasi, J., and Flanagan, E. (2012). 'A survey of chaplains' roles in pediatric palliative care: integral members of the team.' *Journal of Health Care Chaplaincy, 18*, 1–2, 74–93.

Preface

After one of my lectures in Germany, an older woman approached me as if she had seen a miracle. 'Good God, you are alive!' she said. As I smiled at her with some surprise in my eyes, she explained: 'I had read your name before in relation with the *ars moriendi* tradition, but somehow I had concluded that you had been someone who had lived a long time ago, in the Middle Ages.'

In a sense the woman who came up to me was more right than she realized. For many years I had been living in the Middle Ages. Professionally, at least. Having studied theology in the 1980s, I began to work on my dissertation on the theology of Thomas Aquinas (Leget 1997). For many years I read thirteenth-century Latin texts every working day and tortured my mind in order to understand the fine distinctions and deep insights of the Angelic Doctor. I was fascinated with the way Aquinas pushed human thinking to its limits in order to honour God's incomprehensibility. I became convinced that Aquinas had been misinterpreted in later centuries, depicted as the architect of an analogical 'stairway to heaven'. And I considered him to be the best possible guide in answering the central question of my life in those days: What is the relation between life on earth and eternal life?

Why is this important? Because every text is the fruit of a vast and inaccessible process of intertextuality and is written in a specific context. This book is no exception. And in order to understand what I try to do in this book, it is important to explain a little more about its origin.

I was born and raised in the Netherlands and have been living and working there ever since. In the years that I was studying thirteenth-century theology, in twentieth-century Holland a specific culture was being developed with regard to end-of-life issues (Kennedy 2002; Leget 2013a; Schotsmans and Meulenbergs 2005). In the media, fierce debates were being reported that would result in the first legislation worldwide on euthanasia and physician-assisted suicide in 2001. What struck me from a 'medieval' perspective was that in these debates, the proponents of the right to assisted dying tried to exclude any reference to religion or spirituality as much as possible. In a typical Dutch pragmatic way the issue of assisted dying was seen as something that should be settled among free, tolerant citizens, leaving their spiritual convictions in the private sphere. Roughly speaking, among intellectuals, being for euthanasia was considered to be a sign of being enlightened, while having doubts about it or being against it one was suspected to be unreasonable or even religious. The process of dying evolved into a new kind of secular dogmatism.

After obtaining my PhD in 1997 I began doing empirical research in two nursing homes in Rotterdam. My objective was to build a bridge between the end-of-life discussions in the Netherlands and the forgotten wisdom of the Middle Ages. The step of more than seven centuries was a big one, and switching from thirteenth-century texts to twentieth-century patients was both confusing and inspiring. My empirical research consisted of participatory observation.

For many months I was involved in taking care of severely ill and dying patients and I was challenged to reconsider what I had learned from a theoretical perspective until then. And this is where Aquinas turned out to be an unexpected mentor. If I had to summarize two things that I had learned from this medieval author, I should mention his respect for the limits of human rationality and the respect he has for his opponents. In studying theology and philosophy, Aquinas constantly seeks to learn from what he considers to be wrong at first sight. This open mindedness, by the way, caused him many problems in his time.

The more I was involved in the caring of patients and their families, the more I was touched by the importance of openness and inner freedom in order to be really attentive to what people experience. But I also learned that in the face of something so incomprehensible as death our rational mind is constantly inclined to play tricks on us. It is hard to endure the uncertainties and insecurities related to the dying process, but this is perhaps the most humane way to deal with what makes us human beings. This brought me to developing the concept of inner space, a metaphor central to my approach to the dying process. It helped me to deal with the inner polyphony, the many different voices inside us that we experience and encounter when dealing with the close of life.

In the search for a way to develop my thoughts around the concept of inner space, I came across the fifteenth-century *ars moriendi* tradition. This concept appealed to me because of its simplicity and honesty. I was charmed by the idea that this was something designed to help dying patients instead of their caregivers and I soon realized that in contemporary culture we deal with the same big issues, although, of course, framed differently.

By keeping the medieval tensions but transforming them into polyphonies I constructed a framework that was meant to help twenty-first-century patients and formal and informal caregivers to deal with the end of life. My first monograph on this framework was published in 2003 and was updated in 2012. My second book was published in 2008. Both books had many reprints and were received well by both caregivers and the general public (Leget 2003, 2008). I became convinced that the *ars moriendi* model could offer accessible and plain language for addressing the big questions of life and death. For the last two years the model has been used in a number of healthcare facilities in caring practice and education, and it is the subject of scientific research. This publication builds on both Dutch books and other texts that have been written up to this point.

The composition of this book is as follows. In the first chapter the context of Western dying in the twenty-first century is sketched. I will argue that death plays many tricks on us, and much of our culture is trying to pretend that this is not the case. In the second chapter I will focus on the medieval *ars moriendi* tradition as a helpful contrast to our times, from which we can learn. I will argue that in essence as human beings we are still dealing with the same issues as six centuries ago. And although we may have found new solutions, we have also created new problems. Nevertheless, the medieval *ars moriendi* model may help us when we make two important adjustments. The first adjustment is replacing the goal of a blessed death with the concept of inner space. The second adjustment is transforming the binary of heaven and hell with a dialectical tension in which polyphony is allowed with regard to the five important themes central to any *ars moriendi*. The third chapter focuses on the concept of inner space and ways of reaching and promoting it. Chapters 4 to 8 are dedicated to the five themes: autonomy, suffering, saying goodbye, unfinished business and hope. These chapters have a similar structure. Having introduced the theme central to the chapter by means of a case study, I will zoom out and focus on our contemporary culture, in order to show how there is a certain one-sidedness in the way the theme central to this chapter presents itself to us. Reframing this theme in terms of a tension between two opposite poles, we are able to discover how we can develop inner space to deal with the theme. Having discussed all of the five themes in this way, in the ninth chapter I move on to the question of how the *ars moriendi* model can be used from a religious perspective. In the last chapter various ways of working with the *ars moriendi* model will be discussed.

The Dutch have a problem with accepting authority. And although I have already confessed my respect for a thirteenth-century Italian thinker, I am probably more Dutch than I realize. This might help the reader to understand how this book comes across. It does not focus on good and bad, right and wrong, dos and don'ts. My intention is to create a space for reflection that helps to develop inner freedom. I will be critical of tendencies in North Atlantic contemporary culture that deprive us of our inner freedom and are reductionist in their effects on us. In this respect this book does adopt a moral position, and although I do not intend to argue for or against delicate moral issues like euthanasia or assisted dying here, I consider my position far from relativist. For me, the quality of conversation about these issues, the openness and honesty, the inner freedom with which conversations of this kind are held are more important than their outcome.

In the many years that I have been working on this subject my gratitude has been extended to so many people that I do not even dare to try to list names. There is, however, one exception: my great love and inspiration Stephanie Stiel, who offered the space and support that enabled me to write this monograph. I hope that this book is appreciated as a way of expressing my gratitude and will provide a model (that I do not consider to be my intellectual property but that of Western culture) to the people who may benefit from it when facing the end of their life or the end of life of the ones they care for. This includes the many patients I have been working with and who inspired me to write the stories in this book.

In the summer of 2016, in the process of writing this book, my younger sister Angélique ('Liek') was diagnosed with cancer and died unexpectedly after a short period of only one week. The loss is immense. I dedicate this book to her loving memory.

Erlangen en Zeist,
13 July – 7 September 2016,
Carlo Leget

How Death Plays Tricks on Us

According to the ancient Greek philosopher Aristotle – and his theory has been repeated innumerable times by others – death is the greatest evil that can happen to any human being. As always, Aristotle has a point here – at the scale of destructive events that may happen to anyone, death is the most radical one because it is the destruction of the very person. But perhaps we do not need a great mind as ancient as Aristotle's to convince us that death is no good. Everyone who has really loved someone knows by their own experience how deep a wound death can cut. Death is the opposite of life. And although we know that all that lives are born to die, this knowledge does not help us when we suffer a terrible loss. Death makes us suffer and there is no escape.

When one is confronted with the inescapable cruelty of death, it might be a comforting thought that there is something like an *ars moriendi* or art of dying (Laager 1996). The term might have some appeal because it seems to promise that there is a way out of the hopeless situation all human beings are in. If dying can be learned and practised as an art, perhaps death will not be so cruel and horrible. At the same time, the idea of an art of dying may sound ridiculous. How can dealing with our inescapable unhappy end be connected with something as noble as an art? Is perhaps the expression 'art of dying' nothing more than a misleading euphemism? A cheap trick to sell something horrible as something noble?

After one of my lectures a young woman came to me and expressed her astonishment. 'It is peculiar,' she said, 'that one can talk about death but at the same time it seems to be covered by some kind of membrane. It is as if one cannot really touch it. You can try to realize that you will die yourself one day but it remains something far away. Even if you experience someone dying, it is still that other person who dies and not you. Isn't that odd? It seems like we have some innate protection against death.' Without realizing it, this young woman had formulated a thought that had already been expressed by the seventeenth-century writer François Larochefoucauld (2002): 'Neither the sun nor death can be looked at steadily'. Death blinds our rational thinking. Direct confrontation with this theme can only puzzle us. We can only approach it indirectly, as it is reflected in the processes of loss, decay and dying (Dastur 1995; Jankélévich 1966).

Before we begin to develop an art of dying for the twenty-first century, I propose to do something that the French philosopher Paul Ricoeur coined as a 'hermeneutics of suspicion'. In this chapter I want to reflect a little more on the pitfalls and limits of such an enterprise. For there is one thing that I want to avoid at all costs: to offer a beautiful story that only comforts as long as this book is being read, but will prove to be useless when death knocks at our door in real life. Let us therefore take a closer look at what death is and which tricks it plays on us.

Fear of death

People are afraid of dying. It seems to be a natural thing. Death is often associated with pain and suffering, and rightly so. In the dying process we seem to lose everything we have, everything we are. We do not know what is next or, even worse, if there is anything after death at all. Death is avoided in normal conversations. A friend of mine who works in palliative care told me that her parents do not want to talk about her work. When it comes to her professional life a painful silence fills the room. There are things you can talk about, and there are things that should be kept quiet.

But if we are afraid of death, what precisely are we afraid of? Psychologists have been studying fear of death for decades, and a quick look at the scales they use can give us an impression of what is at stake. The Collett-Lester Fear of Death Scale (Collett and Lester 1969), for example, distinguishes between two key dimensions involving death, that both have two sides. The first dimension is the state of death versus the process of dying, and the second dimension concerns one's own death versus the death of others. As such it includes four subscales: death of self (e.g., total isolation of death, shortness of life, never thinking or experiencing), dying of self (e.g., pain involved in dying, intellectual degeneration, lack of control over process, grief of others), death of others (e.g., losing someone close, never being able to communicate again, feeling lonely without the person), dying of others (e.g., watching the person suffer, having to be with someone who is dying).

What we learn from this is that what we normally subsume under the heading of one word consists in fact of a number of phenomena that are closely interrelated and are hard to distinguish as they hypnotize us. Fear of death has many faces and exists in a seemingly endless variety of mixtures and variations. Getting a grip on our fear of death is complex. But there is a second complexity at a deeper level.

When we turn to philosophy we will discover that in existentialism a distinction is made that is even more puzzling than the fear of death scale. In Paul Tillich's classical work *The Courage To Be* (1952), a fundamental distinction is made that is helpful in order to understand why death cannot be looked at steadily: the distinction between fear and anxiety.

Fear is an emotion that has a specific object that can be known, analysed and towards which we can position ourselves. Fear can be overcome by being courageous. Courage is a virtue and, like all virtues, this attitude can be developed and trained by being exposed to the object we fear. Knowledge about the object which is feared is often an important key in developing the virtue of courage. People who fear flying in airplanes, for example, can be informed that airplanes do not fly in a void, but float on air, which has a specific substance just like water does. Knowing that airplanes are 'air borne' may help to take away the feeling of being delivered to something incomprehensible and may help in developing the courage to embark on an aircraft and experience that one can survive this.

The problem with anxiety is that this does not have an object. Or to put it more precisely, the object of anxiety is the negation, the denial of any object. Anxiety is something against which we are powerless and helpless because we cannot grasp it. We cannot analyse it, position ourselves towards it, and there are no virtues that can be developed in this respect. Tillich works out three types of anxiety: that of fate and death (the anxiety of death), that of emptiness and loss of meaning (the anxiety of meaninglessness) and that of guilt and condemnation (the anxiety of condemnation). These three form a permanent existential threat underlying the life we lead. But this threat manifests itself as fear. This is no coincidence: on fear we can get a hold, because it has an object. And this is what we do all the time, out of fear for meaninglessness.

Human beings cannot live without meaning, as Victor Frankl discovered in the hell of Auschwitz (Frankl 2006). We are self-interpreting animals, as the Canadian philosopher Charles Taylor put it (1985). Meaning is what keeps us going and what helps us to deal with what threatens us. Meaning is always there, and although we cannot look steadily at meaninglessness – like we cannot look steadily at death – we can deal with it by identifying how it is reflected in certain phenomena. Dealing with this reflection and fearing it is a natural attitude. And this is not only something we all do as individuals, it is also something very clearly observable in Western society from the Middle Ages until the present day.

Death and society

From the 1950s to the 1980s there seemed to be a general agreement on the fact that death in Western culture was a taboo. The French historian Philippe Ariès had even found names for it in his vast monograph on almost a thousand years of Western European dying (Ariès 1991). After the 'tamed death' of the early Middle Ages, when people felt their last hours approaching in acceptance, in the late Middle Ages it was custom to be focused on 'one's own death' as being the moment of divine judgement. From the early eighteenth century it was the death of the other, 'thy death' that was the focus of attention, culminating in the death cults of Romanticism. From the beginning of the twentieth century, finally death became something shameful, which is expressed by the label 'forbidden death'. More and more the dying process was placed outside the family circle and in the hospital, and life was increasingly seen as something that should be happy. For anything so much related to suffering, decay, sorrow and mourning there was no longer a place in society.

Ariès has been criticized for his nostalgic view on dying in the early Middle Ages among other things, but the point he made about death being banned from society was widely recognized. As early as the 1950s anthropologist Geoffrey Gorer coined the expression 'pornography of death' indicating something which everyone knew was there but no one dared to speak about (Gorer 1965). And until Ernest Becker's famous book *The Denial of Death,* the same message was repeated in many different ways (Becker 1973; Simpson 1979).

In the same years as Ariès wrote his famous work, however, there were influential movements and voices emerging that sang a different tune. In 1967 Dame Cicely Saunders, one of the pioneers of the contemporary palliative care movement, founded St Christopher's Hospice in London. The place became a symbol for a different attitude towards the dying process: no longer shamefully hidden in a hospital where all cards were put on physical cure, but a caring environment where multidisciplinary attention was paid to deal with 'total pain'. In 1969 the Swiss-American psychiatrist Elisabeth Kübler-Ross published her ground-breaking book, *On Death and Dying,* in which she gave voice to the most silenced and hidden group so far: the dying patients (Kübler-Ross 1969). In the last 50 years in many countries palliative care has developed into an impressive movement, bringing back the dying process in society and the community. In many countries palliative medicine has become a medical specialty, and in other countries it is seen as an important dimension of generalist medical care. Does all this mean that death has been 'tamed' again, and we have escaped from the tricks that death plays on us?

Since the end of the 1980s a number of sociologists and anthropologists have written some interesting studies about the way societies and individuals are trapped in the paradoxes that are created by contemporary cultures dealing with death. Tony Walter, for example, in his monograph of the same name speaks of a 'revival of death' supported by more and more experts who know exactly what happens or should happen during the dying process on the one hand, and a movement of ordinary people not claiming any special knowledge but fighting for the right to determine themselves how they will die and be buried or cremated on the other (Walter 1994). Despite all the differences, interestingly, both groups have one thing in common: death is being controlled in one way or another, either by professionalism or by autonomous choice.

Does this mean that after so many centuries we have reached a point where death is no longer denied or forbidden, but integrated and accepted? Sometimes things are more complicated than they may seem on the surface. In order to understand the deeper logic underlying these developments it is helpful to turn to turn to the work of Clive Seale (1998). According to Seale, from a sociological perspective, death causes two problems: the stability of social structures is threatened and the security of our individual existence is shocked. Therefore, culture by definition is a collective effort to turn away from the inevitability of dying – given our corporeal existence – and turn towards life.

In this context it is helpful to distinguish between death as a sociological taboo and death as a psychological taboo. From a sociological perspective it is hard to maintain that death is still a taboo in our society. Death is all around in the media; people die a lot in books, newspapers, TV series and films, and in many societies right-to-die discussions have great visibility in the media and the political arena.

From a psychological perspective, however, death still seems to be something that remains 'covered by some kind of membrane' as the young woman quoted before put it. And the interesting question is whether the efforts to challenge death as a sociological taboo are perhaps expressions that only confirm death as a psychological taboo: as long as I am reading, writing and talking about the death of other people, I do not have to confront my own mortality. As long as I am fighting for my right to die, I can ease myself with the illusion that I control death, and death does not control me. The tricks that death plays on us are of a very subtle kind.

Thus, although death as a sociological taboo and death as a psychological taboo can be distinguished, they are also interrelated. According to Seale, three concepts are helpful to understand our culture in the way it pretends to have death under control. The first concept is that of imagined communities. For centuries the majority of people who lived in Europe have been part of such a community that helped in dealing with mortality. The Roman Catholic Church, for example, considers itself a 'communion of saints', a spiritual union of both the living and the dead members of the Church, of those on earth, in heaven, and, for those who believe in purgatory, those who are in that state of purification. However painful and sad a dying process might be, one does not fall out of this imagined community, and still belongs to the Church at all times. Moreover, this union offers the possibility of remaining in contact by remembrance, prayer and rituals. During the Mass on Sunday, the lines between the living and the dead are crossed: the people attending church become part of the Last Supper that took place 2000 years ago in Jerusalem, and people from the local community who have died recently are prayed for and remembered.

Although religion may be the most explicit and sophisticated way of an imagined community helping to cope with death, society offers many more of these. In times of conflict and war nationalism is an important source for making sense of the absurdity of people killing people they don't even personally know. Those who have died for their country are praised and remembered, their names are carved in stone in order to express that their sacrifice will never be forgotten. The pain of families missing a loved one is compensated by being connected to a 'higher cause', the imagined community of a nation.

But also in ordinary life we are part of many imagined communities, like, for example, that of healthcare as an institution. Medicine tells you how to lead a healthy life. If anything goes wrong, medicine is there to cure you. If that does not work, medicine is there to care for you, to ease your pain, to alleviate your suffering. And if the dying process begins, again the physician will take control – either by palliative care or assisted dying – and sign the official death certificate. Medicine is built on science. Science is rational and objective. Rationality and objectivity enable predictability and control. Life and death are under control.

Next to the idea of imagined communities – and the examples can be extended to life insurances, risk calculations, statistical groups and state policy – Seale introduces a second concept: the hope of revivalism.

The term stems from Tony Walter and refers to the idea that death should not be regarded as a taboo, but as an opportunity for growth (Walter 1994). Dying and bereavement are seen as special chances for personal development. Ideas about what is healthy and normal come into existence and reframe the experiences of people.

One of the most well-known examples of this mechanism is the way the ideas of Elisabeth Kübler-Ross about five stages of grief (denial, anger, depression, bargaining, acceptance) have influenced how people interpreted their own process (Kübler-Ross 1969). Acceptance became interpreted as being the last and final stage of grief, a stage that had a normative appeal because dying in acceptance seemed to be the task that every dying and grieving person should try to reach.

The same implicit normativity is connected to the third concept that Seale introduces in order to understand how societies try to conquer death: resurrective practices (Seale 1998). With this he refers to all kinds of practices and customs that are aimed at maintaining life and suppressing death. These practices do not frame the dying process as a natural event, but as a project or inner adventure that we have to undertake in order to reach atonement and fulfilment. The good death is a strong, autonomous death. Analysing an interview on national television with the terminally ill Dennis Potter, Seale shows how the famous playwright is depicted as an adventurer who is determined to make his last journey of discovery. None of the decay, the tarnish and the process of surrendering are shown, but the courage, curiosity and vitality of life.

The opposite of such a successful death is found in the individuals who die in desolate loneliness; the people who are not able to make their own choices; severely ill patients who do not succeed in being approachable because they are awfully malformed by their disease or stink too much because of the horrible cancer process that irrevocably pushes them to the margins of social acceptability. These are the cases that we do not want to see. They are not shown on television or in newspapers, and confront us with a side of the dying process that does not fit in any of the strategies mentioned before.

But haven't we stated before that we do have an answer to cases like these in the form of palliative care as an approach that seeks to be a safety net for all those who run the risk of not fitting into the mainstream picture of acceptable dying? The question is whether there are limits even to the palliative care approach, limits that challenge our efforts to control or tame death and leave us in a state of confusion. An interesting perspective on this has been provided by an original study by Julia Lawton.

Death and the body

Julia Lawton studied patients' experiences of palliative care and discovered some interesting ambivalences that give us food for thought (Lawton 1998, 2000). They are helpful in our hermeneutics of suspicion that should guard us from designing a contemporary *ars moriendi* that is naive about the tricks that death plays on us. Her central proposition accords well with what we have learned from the work of Clive Seale. According to Lawton, the hospice movement in the UK is so popular because it presents an image of death that many people would like to consume: death as something that can be transformed into a last event of self-expression and self-exposition. Lawton opposes this image because she thinks it does not represent the experiences and struggles of real patients. The question then is, how can an approach that is designed to support dying patients and their families lead to practices that fail to reach this goal?

As a researcher, Lawton does not want to cast blame on people. She wants to understand how good intentions seem to meet unexpected and often unwanted boundaries. The problem, in her view, is that in Western culture there is a dominant idea of the human person as a rational mind that uses a body to express itself. And although palliative care is based on a holistic anthropology, in essence its nature is dualistic, separating the mind from the body and valuing the former over the latter. A question that is unthinkable for palliative care is, for example, whether sometimes the body presents a non-negotiable lower limit beyond which life is no longer living. This question is unthinkable because when we locate the centre of personhood in the mind, and separate it from the body, the body is strictly speaking not needed for life to be valuable, let alone set limits to the life of the mind. Think of Plato's saying that the body is a prison of the soul.

In order to understand the perspective of the dying person, Lawton says, we need a different anthropology. We should instead follow the French philosopher Maurice Merleau-Ponty (1945), who claims that we not only have a body (the object body), but we also are a body (the subject body). Both perspectives of the body are important to keep in mind, and the great problem for our rational mind is to understand how they can both be true at the same time. We are who we are by the way our lived body is in the world. And who and what we are is not so much dependent on what we think, as on what we can do. The more patients are frustrated and limited in what they can do or in their ability to live life freely, the more their identity is threatened. More and more the subject body itself is experienced as an object body.

Lawton gives some concrete examples of the frictions that may occur in palliative care. In order to live as actively as possible until the end, patients are encouraged to perform activities. Many patients, however, do not want this: being so much limited in their abilities they no longer feel they are the same person they used to be. The same mechanism is reflected in dying patients who give away personal belongings because they can no longer identify with them.

Another example of the frictions and paradoxes that exist is the fact that dying patients feel safer in small rooms, because they are no longer able to master larger spaces. Moreover, the confrontation with larger spaces painfully reminds them of who they once were and who they have now lost.

According to Lawton, palliative care does not know how to deal with the experiences of dying patients who feel that their subject body is being changed into an object body. Unintentionally and inevitably this process is confirmed by the caregiver. The more caregivers take over from patients, the more patients feel their experience of being an object body, a burden, confirmed. When patients, as a result of this, do not want to live any longer, how should we then interpret this as caregivers? Are we secretly offended that despite our efforts and perhaps the satisfaction with ourselves a patient really does not want to live any longer? Do we have doubts about ourselves for having unconsciously sent signals that the patient's life is no longer worth living? Do we as caregivers subconsciously send signals of being happy not to be in the place of the one we care for in their last days?

One of the most shocking cases Lawton discusses is the story of Annie, a 67-year-old women who suffered from a severe cervical cancer. Due to a number of complications she could not hold her faeces and urine and this caused a terrible penetrating odour which could be smelled up to the reception desk of the hospice. Burning aromatic oils did not change anything for the better and caregivers, family members and other patients started to complain. No other patient wanted to be in the room with her, but Annie did not want to lie alone in a room, as she was afraid of being lonely. Annie asked for terminal sedation, and with reduced consciousness she spent the last two weeks of her life in a separate room where it smelled terribly and her family no longer visited her.

Lawton is not interesting blaming and shaming or telling people what is right and wrong. She wants to investigate what we can learn about our society from extreme cases like this. In her view, we have become used to seeing human beings as stable, bounded and autonomous individuals. When people become so ill that their body is falling apart, our culture does not know how to respond. Leaking faeces and urine is shameful and associated with loss of personal dignity. One is reduced to the status of a young child not yet capable of control over bladder and bowels. But Annie's case was worse: she transgressed all possible boundaries when her odour penetrated into the noses of other people. She could not be kept at a distance and forced herself on everyone.

Looking at the history of Western Europe, we will discover that intolerance towards anyone or anything stinking has increased enormously during the last century. In earlier centuries the world was full of unpleasant odours, and faeces was not considered to be something that should be hidden (Süsskind 1985). As we now live in an age of great intolerance in these matters, it is hardly conceivable how people lived and died in earlier days.

What is the role of the hospice in all this? Lawton points to the fact that the hospice is caught up in a mechanism that unintentionally runs against her mission to integrate death into society. The good thing is that the hospice functions as a place where even those people can be cared for, those for whom there is no other place in society, such as people who leak bodily juices. By offering a solution to this problem, however, the hospice confirms that this is a problem and it even helps to keep those people out of sight of society. Socially, Annie had been dead for two weeks before her heart stopped beating. By helping to conceal patients like Annie, the hospice unintentionally helps to keep intact the image of decent dying of stable, bounded and autonomous individuals.

Dealing with ambivalence

We come to the close of our chapter on the tricks death plays on us. Everything that lives is born to die. By being corporeal creatures, human beings are vulnerable and subjected to mortality. The inevitability of death causes an existential anxiety that is so hard to deal with that it expresses itself in the many forms of fear of death. Society offers many strategies to deal with these fears and covers up the psychological taboo by attacking the social taboo on death. But however much imagined communities, revivalism and resurrective practices may help to foster the illusion that we control death, in the end we remain vulnerable corporeal beings that are not able to look steadily into the black sun of death.

What have we learned in this chapter that we will take to heart in the developments of our contemporary *ars moriendi*? In the first place, we may conclude that no *ars moriendi* can take away the mystery of death.

Rational control of death is an illusion and the art of dying should rather be an art of being open to tensions and ambivalences than trying to resolve them or rationalize them away.

A second lesson that we will take to heart is that contrary to the many ways in which our culture tries to have active control over death, our *ars moriendi* should be open to undergoing and enduring what cannot be solved.

A third lesson we have learned is that there is a great deal of implicit and explicit normativity – dos and don'ts, rights and wrongs – in the way our culture deals with the dying process. Our *ars moriendi* should be wary of high ideals and practise the virtue of humility. For the sake of the vulnerability of dying patients and their families, all heroism and romanticism about dying should be avoided, also in their moral versions. We want to start with what is there, being open to learn new things in every encounter.

In the next chapter we will begin to develop our new *ars moriendi* by looking back to a particular *ars moriendi* tradition that runs back to the Middle Ages. As the French say, *Reculer pour mieux sauter*: stepping back in order to jump further. By studying a model that has been proved by many generations of our predecessors over more than five centuries, we hope to build on solid ground.

The Art of Dying

For more than twenty centuries, dying has been considered as an important event that one should prepare for. From ancient Greek and Roman literature until the nineteenth century many thinkers have contributed to the body of literature that was known as *ars moriendi*, the art of dying (Bayard 1999; Girard-Augry 1986, Laager 1996). The great philosopher Plato had already described the main task of philosophy as meditating about death. Christianity took up this thought and reframed it in terms of being ultimately connected with God after death. Remnants of how our ancestors were preoccupied with their mortality can still be found. In the Middle Ages, for example, people feared an unforeseen death. In many of the great European cathedrals a statue of Saint Christopher can be seen at the entrance. He should guard people from dying without preparation. A death without preparation was seen as a death without the ability to confess one's sins, and therefore a single ticket to hell.

As medical science progressed, the dying process became more and more medicalized. What happened to the dying person was reframed in medical terms, and in the first half of the twentieth century, death was increasingly seen as a medical failure, a problem that could be solved with the help of science in the future. People do not like to expose their failures, so death was kept away, and the palliative care movement can be seen as an attempt to bring back dying patients into the community. As palliative care aims at total care for patient and family, and pays attention to the physical, psychosocial and spiritual dimension of the dying process, one might think that it could be seen as a contemporary art of dying. In the light of the old *ars moriendi* tradition, however, three things give food for thought.

In the first place, where the *ars moriendi* tradition was set up around the patient as subject and apprentice, palliative care is defined from the perspective of the caregiver. Palliative care consists of practices in which formal and informal caregivers work hard to enable other people to die well. The *ars moriendi* tradition, however, was a spiritual practice of those who were preparing for their own death.

In the second place, it is striking that the dimension that has traditionally been at the centre of the dying process has shifted to the margins; spiritual care is an accepted dimension of palliative care, but the one that is the least integrated into the medical framework and the one that is still most in development. And although there have been major breakthroughs in the past ten years, in many contexts spiritual care is still underdeveloped or marginally integrated (Puchalski *et al.* 2009, 2014).

In the third place, in the best cases spiritual care in palliative care concerns people with incurable diseases. In the majority of cases, however, the people cared for are terminally ill. The ancient *ars moriendi* traditions, however, were seen as an *ars vivendi*, an art of living: preparing for death as a way of life, for healthy people as well, because what is really worth living for is discovered best in the light of one's mortality.

In this book we aim to develop an *ars moriendi* which can also be seen as an *ars vivendi*: a spiritual framework that helps patients and formal and informal caregivers to meet and discuss what it means to die and what is needed to die in a meaningful way. It is not presented as an alternative to palliative care, but as a framework that can be used in palliative care, integrating the spiritual dimension into physical and psychosocial care. In order to do so we will first take a step back and look in the mirror of history.

The medieval *ars moriendi* tradition

In the years 1346–53 a mortal disease later called 'the Black Death' spread over Europe, killing an estimated fifty million people, which was about sixty per cent of the population of that time. People died within a week, and nothing could be done. In terms of death numbers, this epidemic of bubonic plague was the greatest tragedy Europe has witnessed, surpassing every war before and after.

The Black Death was the cause of an innumerable amount of personal tragedies. It disrupted medieval society and traumatized Western culture for decades. The dance of death or 'dance macabre', consisting of dancing skeletons including people from all levels of society, is among the most well-known heritages of this collective trauma.

The Black Death, however, was also considered to be a spiritual disaster, because it prevented people from preparing well for the transition between earthly life and the hereafter. In particular, when the clergy were among the first to die from the plague, the remaining population was left spiritually abandoned. As a result of this, in decades following the Black Death, block prints were manufactured, accompanied by texts for the few who were able to read, that showed five scenes in which a dying man was depicted in his spiritual struggle (Bayard 1999; Girard-Augry 1986).

The structure of the scenes was always the same. On one side of the bed devils and demons were trying to tempt the dying person and convince him that everything he had believed so far could not help him now. At the other side of the bed saints and angels were at pains to inspire the moribund with virtuous thoughts that were meant as an antidote to the temptations. On the last picture there was always a priest holding a candle and a crucifix, comforting the dying man, and one would see how the soul left the body and an angel would take him to heaven.

Although the order and list of temptations was not always the same, medieval pragmatism made sure that there were always five temptations, so that anyone could easily remember them looking at the fingers on one hand. What then were these temptations and why were these five so important for medieval people to resist?

Normally the first attack of the devils would be aimed at the moribund's faith. Faith is seen as the foundation of religion and attacking this foundation is the most effective and efficient way of destroying everything that is built on it. The weapon used by the devils is doubt. There is no heaven, no hell, no Last Judgement. Every human life has the same outcome: death. Nothing more. On the block prints we see the devils holding up a blanket, keeping out of sight the spiritual world of angels and saints. There is just suffering and the here and now. So why not give up on all of this and end one's life right away? But then the angels come into play. And in a next woodcut we see them encourage the moribund to hold on to his faith and stay connected with God. Of course, one cannot prove that there is a heaven and a hell, but this is precisely what faith is about: to have confidence in what cannot be seen and trust God that he will not abandon those who call for him.

If faith is preserved amid the suffering, the devils start their second attack: the temptation of desperation. For if there is a God and a heaven in which all tears will be dried, how realistic is it that one will reach such a blessed place? Isn't heaven a place for saints? And how many times did the dying person transgress the Ten Commandments in his life? On the block prints we see a 'helpful' devil holding up a list of sins that have been noted during his lifetime: money that was gained in an unjust way, women that the moribund had had fantasies about, or even worse... And again on the next picture we see the angels coming in with the virtue of hope. They stress that God's misery and love are endlessly greater than any sinfulness human beings might invent. Moreover, one doesn't have to merit access to heaven on one's own. Christ died for our sins and bought us free. So stay hopeful for hope is the anchor of salvation. At the head of the bed we see a cock sitting, symbolizing Saint Peter. Every medieval soul knew what this meant: if the disciple who had betrayed Christ three times had still been worthy enough to receive the keys to the kingdom of heaven, wouldn't there be hope for every sinner?

If faith has been preserved and hope for forgiveness has been rekindled, the foundation for a good death seems to be there. But dying is not just being directed to a life to come, it is also letting go of everything one has become attached to in one's life on earth. The next attack of the devils focuses precisely on this attachment, which is called avarice in medieval terms. On the block prints we see a beautiful house with a great wine cellar, wife and children, horses, and devils who formulate uneasy thoughts about who will live there after one has died, enjoying the company of one's wife and children. But then again the angels come into play, and this time they are holding up the blanket. Whoever focuses too much on what keeps them connected to this earthly existence will never be able to let go of life. Therefore the blanket is used to keep all loved ones out of sight. It is important to focus on the spiritual world and the things to come. Opposed to avarice is the virtue of charity, which connects the dying soul first and foremost to God, and only after this and through this, with all earthly persons and matters.

After the attempts to undermine the three central virtues of faith, hope and charity, the devils seem to slowly run out of options to win the battle. So they put all their cards on the intensity of the pain and suffering of the dying person. Why suffer so much? Why not put an end to all misery simply by taking one's life as the Romans and other pagans would do? The temptation of impatience is fuelled by thought about injustice: I do not deserve this, this is inhumane. Again the angels try to comfort the moribund by offering an impressive counter story: look at how Christ died, look at all martyrs who have died for their faith and see what they have achieved. Suffering is a temptation we all have to undergo, and which can be used for purification and to strengthen the relationship with God. In order to illustrate this on the block prints we see a number of saints who are depicted holding their cause of death: Saint Barbara with the tower from which she was thrown, Saint Lawrence with the grill on which he was burned, and many others.

The last attack of the devils is a wonderful piece of medieval psychology. Anyone who has been able to resist the first four temptations must be proud of this achievement, and rightly so. This time the tactic of the devils is in line with this pride. They praise the moribund and tell him how great he is so that his pride may develop into complacency. And when the dying person thinks he is sure to be worthy of entering heaven, the devils have won the battle. For complacency – not respecting your place in the order of creation – is seen as the root of all sin. Because Adam and Eve were complacent, not obeying God's prohibition to eat from the tree of life, they were thrown out of the Garden of Eden. Humility is the key to religious life: accepting that it is not one's own merit to have resisted all temptations the devils have presented, but God's grace that has given you this strength.

Limitations and possibilities

The medieval *ars moriendi* is attractive because of its simplicity: all struggles of the dying process are summarized into five choices. It is clear what should be avoided and what should be done. Considering the psychological intelligence of the devils there seems to be a great amount of experiential knowledge incorporated in this medieval model. Nevertheless, there are some serious reasons why the medieval *ars moriendi* cannot be transferred to the twenty-first century without running into serious problems.

The first problem is that the model can only work in a predominantly Christian culture. It presupposes a shared cultural and religious horizon that becomes increasingly rare, especially in a world where more and more people from various cultural and religious backgrounds live together. But also for many people who are inspired by the Christian tradition, when it comes to their spiritual guidance the medieval *ars moriendi* is not so helpful any more. Contemporary Christian faith is not so much focused on heaven and hell as the faith of our medieval predecessors was. And the way their struggles have been framed is too rigid and black and white to be convincing and inspiring in our day. The dying process looks almost like a final exam for heaven instead of a valuable process in which humaneness is shared among all those who are involved. And finally, the medieval *ars moriendi* is too much focused on salvation of the soul, without paying attention to the corporeal and psychosocial dimension of the dying process.

A contemporary art of dying asks for different accents. To begin with, it should be a framework that is open to a great variety of spiritual traditions, religious and non-religious. Moreover, it should be designed in such a way that the spiritual dimension can play an integrating role among the other three dimensions of palliative care. This would mean that the process of dying becomes more important than the outcome of heaven or hell. And finally, such an *ars moriendi* should be no straitjacket, but a model that offers space for the countless personal ways of dying in our time. But how do we create such an *ars moriendi* and where do we start?

Before we judge too harshly about the medieval *ars moriendi*, we might perhaps take a second look at the block prints. For, are we sure we really have grasped the spiritual depth and scope of this model? Considering that the model has been copied and used for centuries and has been helpful for millions of people who died before us, could it be that we are too quick in our judgement?

Perhaps our first interpretation of the block prints was too much from an outsider's perspective and too superficial to really understand why it was so helpful and appealing to our medieval predecessors.

Maybe understanding its real value is only possible when we try to approach it from the side of the spiritual process it was part of. Interpreting the model within the framework of Christian spirituality, we might discover that the model had its place and function in the context of a lived relationship with God. Within this context, the dying process would appear as a process of transformation. Perhaps the real power of the medieval *ars moriendi* was located in the fivefold transformation into a form of surrender that was evoked by the dialectical process of angels responding to devils. Could it be that the angels were comforting the dying with admonitions that might sound as follows when translated into twenty-first-century language?

- Do not clasp to what the human eye can see or measure. Trust that there is much more between heaven and earth than fits in your head (Faith).

- Do not fixate on what went wrong in the past. Do not fixate on feelings of guilt. Be mild towards yourself. Have faith that you will be looked on with love (Hope).

- Do not cling on to what you have gathered in your life. It aggravates the pain of dying. Let go and focus on where you are expected (Love).

- Resist the restrictions of being identical with your pain and suffering. You are more and bigger than your pain. Have faith that the pain will end (Patience).

- Do not fight to preserve your achievements, your decorum, your pride. There is nothing more to prove. Do not pretend to be bigger than you are (Humility).

If we look to the block prints from this angle, we can see how there might be an effort to comfort and pacify the dying person. The five big themes are represented at the close of life in order to achieve acceptance and surrender. The demonic voices try to fixate the moribund with hopelessness, guilt, fear, pain and pride. The angelic voices try to create perspective and space so that the dying person is able to relax and let go.

In the Middle Ages the idea of surrender has the character of entrusting oneself to the loving hands of God. The surrounding framework of the religious tradition was aimed at helping human beings to direct to the invisible and incomprehensible mystery that is the origin and final end of everything. But in essence, the entire spiritual transformation is a process of openness and surrendering. And perhaps this essence can still be of great value for those who live in the twenty-first century, regardless of whether they consider themselves religious or non-religious.

The discovery of inner space

As with every art, the art of dying can only be learned in practice. In one of the nursing homes where I did participatory observation research for some months, I discovered a concept that worked so powerfully – but was yet so normal – that I gradually became convinced that it could help to play a central role in a contemporary *ars moriendi*. During multidisciplinary team meetings it struck me that regularly the word 'space' was used. When discussing a case the caregivers often searched for creating space in the way people experienced themselves or other people. Often this process was accompanied by better communication between those involved, and insight into the questions behind the questions.

One of the patients I met during my research was a widowed woman in her mid-eighties. Suffering from a gastric cancer, she was admitted to the nursing home because she could no longer take care of herself. As the physician entered the room in order to introduce herself, the woman immediately asked her in a demanding tone whether she was prepared to 'help' her if the pain became unbearable. She told the physician that she had a euthanasia declaration in her purse and wanted to be sure that she was treated by a physician who was not afraid of honouring her wishes.

How to respond in such a situation? In a situation like this many things happen in just a few seconds. Witnessing the demanding attitude of the patient and knowing that euthanasia was a very unlikely scenario in a Roman Catholic nursing home at a time where this practice was condoned under certain circumstances but not officially legalized in my country, I experienced feelings of irritation and resistance in myself. I thought it was rude to open a conversation with a physician you do not even know by asking her about something as hard and drastic as active termination of her life. I wondered whether the physician would feel the same and how she would respond. If she turned down this scenario from the very beginning it would be hard to build up a good relationship with her patient. But if she acted as if there were room for this outcome, she would probably have to disappoint her patient at a later phase.

To my surprise, the physician did not choose either of these two options, but responded that euthanasia literally meant 'good death' and that different people understood different things by this term. Reflecting on a good death, she as a physician would think of everything that could be achieved through good palliative care, as she was used to providing with an interdisciplinary team of colleagues. She started to sketch what options would be possible in order to make life bearable and worth living until the end. But, she continued, other people use the term active termination of life by a physician at the explicit request of the patient. The older woman was visibly intrigued by the options that had been sketched some minutes before, which she clearly had not imagined to exist. She asked the physician to tell her some more about this palliative care scenario and after the physician had given some more information, she fell silent. The physician looked at the woman and told her she had a question as well. She would like to know what had made her fill in the euthanasia declaration. What had happened that had brought her to do this? The woman began to talk about her husband, who had suffered from lung cancer and severe breathlessness. It was so hard to bear for her and her children that she had promised herself that she would fill in the declaration form in order to have a way out. The more she spoke about her husband, the more her tone softened and gradually she was able to speak about what she feared most.

Reflecting on this encounter, I was amazed by what had happened because of the way the nursing home physician had responded. Within a few moments the demanding older woman had transformed into a vulnerable and sympathetic grandmother. I also was ashamed of the complicated way the conversation would have developed had I been in the physician's place. The open attitude of the physician had obviously created an atmosphere of trust and attention that enabled the women to open up. By answering the woman's closed question with an open question herself, she managed to create space in the conversation. But the root of this was the space in herself that made her listen without prejudice or judgement.

This is nothing new, of course, in communication training or psychotherapy. But it might be something very fruitful and liberating when adopted as a spiritual attitude.

Reflecting more on what had happened I began to recognize this inner attitude more and more in good communication I observed in the nursing home. Back in my study, I also began to recognize it in a variety of spiritual traditions. I coined it as 'inner space', a metaphor for a state of mind in which one is able to experience a number of thoughts, emotions, impulses, feelings and so on, without identifying with them or being swept away by them. It is a quality that has great impact on the way one experiences the world. And because of this impact it also changes the way one communicates with others.

What then might be the difference between inner space as a spiritual attitude and as a communication technique? As a communication technique, inner space can be seen as a way of emptying oneself in order to be able to reflect the expressions of one's conversation partner as well as possible. As a spiritual attitude, inner space can be seen as a way of connecting with one's inner life and discovering the many inner voices that inhabit us. The self is basically polyphonic and being open to this polyphony can be a great gift to oneself. It can also be a gift to other people when it is used in communication. This brings us back to the voices of the angels and devils in the medieval *ars moriendi*.

Retrieving the *ars moriendi* tradition

In search of a contemporary *ars moriendi*, the concept of inner space might be helpful as a centre that is not exclusively connected to one religious tradition. Putting the concept of inner space at the centre of our *ars moriendi* enables people from whatever spiritual tradition to join in. But what about the five choices that were central to the medieval *ars moriendi*? Are they exclusively and essentially Christian by their very nature, or do they also have a broader anthropological basis which is open to people from other spiritual traditions?

The discovery and framing of the concept of inner space took place in a dialectical process. On the one hand, there was the attempt to understand the five choices of the *ars moriendi* at a deeper level. Reinterpreting the choices from the perspective of a process of transformation to being connected with and surrendering to God, we discovered that the angels and saints were trying to create space, and liberate from feelings that are oppressive. On the other hand, there was the discovery of the concept of space in the conversations at a palliative care unit in a nursing home. Both processes seemed to be analogous in a way, and this strengthened the idea of trying to retrieve the medieval *ars moriendi* tradition by putting the metaphor of inner space at its centre.

If the essence of inner space is being open to the polyphony inside oneself, at first sight the medieval *ars moriendi* seems to connect very well with this idea. The mix of angelic and demonic voices form a confusing choir that represents the many voices that can be heard in many dying patients. There are, however, two problems related to the dualistic nature of the medieval model.

The first problem is related to the fact that the angels are obviously right and the devils are clearly wrong. The medieval model is a highly moralistic model in which good and bad have been well defined beforehand. The road to heaven is narrow but clear. Acting morally right is like following a road map and staying on the road (Mahoney 1987). As a result of this, all human experiences are interpreted in terms of what is on the road map. This is a highly reductionist and deductive way of dealing with morality. It does not allow new experiences to be integrated in moral deliberation: the map has already been drawn, and those who use the map are not entitled to change it.

One might argue that the concept of inner space does not necessarily conflict with the idea of the road map. Using the road map one might still be sensitive to the many voices inside oneself, and this might even help to know which temptations require the strongest avoidance or correction. In this way, however, the concept of inner space is not understood and used consistently. It is used instrumentally for the sake of its sensitivity to polyphony. In that case its fundamental openness is not appreciated. When inner space is sought and appreciated in its radical form, it opens up to new experiences, new insights, new discoveries. It is connected with the capacity to wonder (Hansen 2012). Taking inner space seriously, one must be careful to give words to experiences, being cautious not to frame an experience too quickly and fixate and close off its possible meanings.

The second problem is related to the fact that in every one of the five struggles a clear choice has to be made. One has to choose between one side or the other. There is only black or white, and all shades of grey seem to be filtered out. Following the image of the road map there might be no problem at all with this dualistic approach: one is either following one road or the other. No one can walk on two roads at the same time. The question is, however, whether the road map is the best way of looking at moral life. If we consider moral life, for example as an acorn developing into an oak tree, a completely different approach to morality comes to the fore (Mahoney 1987).

In this approach there is a vision of a certain end as well – the full-grown oak tree – but the road leading to this end is understood as an organic process in which the next best step is discovered only during the process itself.

Does this mean that in the end the *ars moriendi* model we are developing is extremely individualistic and relativistic? Not at all. In order to keep the new *ars moriendi* as open as possible, the two poles of the model should not be formulated in terms of good and bad. The poles should be considered as general anthropological categories that are clear enough to organize our experiences and thoughts, but open enough to not limit and close down on beforehand the interpretation of what we experience. If the model is used in real life, its moral directedness will be influenced by the context in which it is used. This is completely in accordance with the idea of inner space. The practice of palliative care is not a morally neutral practice and thus the moral ideas implicit in concrete palliative care practices – differing in different parts of the world – will also inform the way the *ars moriendi* model works out. Oak trees in southern Europe have a different shape and form from oak trees in the United Kingdom or the United States.

My own development as an ethicist has brought me from the work of Aquinas to care ethics as an interdisciplinary field of studies aimed at forming 'a life-sustaining web of relations' (Tronto 1993). What is considered to be life sustaining will be different in different parts of the world, depending on the 'moral understandings' that are shared (Walker 2007). In the process of discovering this there are a number of more or less well-defined elements that harmonize very well with palliative care philosophy, such as an inductive, practice-oriented approach, a view of human beings as intrinsically relational beings with a great sensitivity to power relations.

The five struggles revisited

We are now in a position to turn to the medieval *ars moriendi* again and ask ourselves how the five struggles could be reframed so that they might be helpful for the struggles people in the twenty-first century encounter. In the Middle Ages, faith was the foundation of the model, and therefore the first attack of the devils was on what people believed in. In contemporary culture one would rather say that patient's autonomy is the foundation of dying well. At first sight one might ask whether any connection at all can be made between this theme and the medieval *ars moriendi*. When we reverse the medieval order of the five struggles, however, an interesting perspective arises.

The last struggle of the medieval *ars moriendi* was between complacency and humility. Interestingly, both have to do with the way one looks at oneself. People who are complacent are satisfied with themselves and do not need anyone else. They are independent and very sure of themselves, very well connected to themselves and to their own perspective on things. No one needs to tell or teach them anything. They know exactly what they want and what is right and wrong. Such people are a closed self, not open to uneasiness, doubt or dialogue. Humility, however, is the reverse of such an attitude. Humility is related to the Latin word 'humus' which means earth. A humble person has both feet on the ground and knows their place in the order of things. Such a person knows themselves by situating themselves in between other people. Although semantically very close, humility has nothing to do with being humiliated. Being humble means being open to dialogue and learning new things.

Complacency and humbleness were moral categories. When we try to reframe them in non-moral categories we can identify the poles of 'oneself' and 'the others'.

The complacent person is self-satisfied, the humble person defines themselves in relation to the others. Both poles are also recognizable in contemporary theories about the human self, and help in forming a background for thinking about autonomy, which is literally speaking nothing more than 'self-governance'. Thus the first question of our new *ars moriendi* model becomes: 'Who am I and what do I really want?' This is a question that can be answered by situating the many voices inside oneself between the poles of 'oneself' and 'the others'.

The penultimate struggle in the medieval model concerned pain and suffering. Here the alternatives were to be either patient or impatient. Again we see a highly moral opposition between a virtue and a vice. Trying to grasp the non-moral content inside these two alternatives one could say that patience is marked by undergoing and enduring, whereas impatience is associated with taking action and doing something about the situation. Doing and undergoing are two non-moral categories that are very helpful in reflecting on the contemporary complexity to deal with pain and suffering amid a great number of medical and technical possibilities. So the second central question of the new *ars moriendi* would be: 'How do I deal with suffering?' This is a question that can be answered by investigating how the many voices inside oneself oscillate between doing and undergoing.

The third struggle in the medieval *ars moriendi* concerned all the good things in life and the alternatives of avarice and charity. Deconstructing this vice and this virtue in non-moral terms, it is clear that both deal with the tension between holding on and letting go. Holding on to all the good things in life, one would never be able to die well. So the medieval solution was to focus on God, keeping all earthly attachments out of sight (remember the angel holding up the blanket) and letting go of the good things in life. In our new *ars moriendi* the poles of holding on and letting go are still valuable, but not as alternatives. The central question: 'How do I say goodbye?' prepares the way for an answer in the tension between these poles, but in a very specific process. As we will see in later chapters, letting go can sometimes only be possible if it is transformed into holding on in a different way.

The second struggle in the Middle Ages centred around the temptation of despair and the virtue of hope. Looking back on one's life and realizing how much has gone wrong, one might be convinced that having such a past there could be no future with God. Looking at the non-moral core of this, one could say that despair is characterized by the destructive power the past can have. By remembering what went wrong in the past, people are chained to something they cannot change. In this situation, the only way to open up a future is to forget about the past. Remembering and forgetting are two non-moral concepts: they can be part of both good and bad practices or actions. The fourth question of our new *ars moriendi* therefore is: 'How do I look back on my life?' This is a question to be answered in the space that is opened up by the poles of remembering and forgetting.

The first struggle in the medieval model, finally, was dedicated to the opposition between faith and loss of faith. Again, the moral content of the opposition was crystal clear. The first struggle decided whether one entered or left the *ars moriendi*. Loss of faith meant that all other struggles would be radically different as well. Deconstructing the virtue of faith, one could say that it deals with having confidence in things that cannot be seen or proven. Faith is about the foundations of our knowledge and the question of what forms of knowledge we consider to be reliable. 'In God we trust, all others must bring data,' is a famous saying of W. Edwards Deming. And with this he very succinctly formulated the two ways in which people seek for epistemological security in our days: either by looking for knowledge based on scientific evidence or by knowledge based on faith. The fifth question of our contemporary *ars moriendi* concerns the way we seek an epistemological hold in matters that do not fit in our heads. The central question here is: 'What can I hope for?' and it is answered between the poles of knowing and believing.

In this chapter we started with studying the medieval *ars moriendi* tradition in order to see whether it could enable us to design an *ars moriendi* model for the twenty-first century. In order for it to be fit to serve the struggles of our contemporaries, we proposed some fundamental changes, although we left the polyphonic five-fold structure intact. At the centre of the new *ars moriendi* we proposed to locate the concept of inner space. In the next chapter we will focus on this central metaphor in order to grasp its importance for the new *ars moriendi*. Following that, in the remaining chapters we will turn back to the five central questions and work out in more detail how they may help with the spiritual struggles people at the end of their lives may go through.

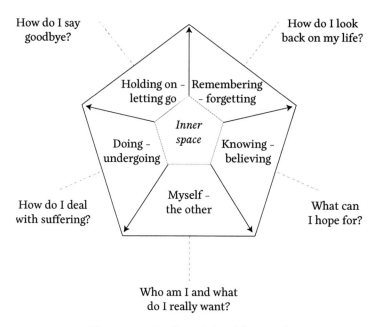

How do I say
goodbye?

How do I look
back on my life?

Holding on -
letting go

Remembering
- forgetting

*Inner
space*

Doing -
undergoing

Knowing -
believing

How do I deal
with suffering?

Myself -
the other

What can
I hope for?

Who am I and what
do I really want?

The *ars moriendi* model or 'diamond'
Leget 2003/2012, 2008

3

Inner Space

Marie de Hennezel worked as a psychologist with terminally ill patients in a hospital in Paris. In her book, *Intimate Death*, she tells a personal story of a friend of hers who had made up his mind to end his life (Hennezel 1998). His parents had been suffering from dementia at old age and he was determined not to follow them on this road. He had taken up the idea of ending his life at the age of 65. He wanted to live as fully as possible until that age, and then he would end his life. There was only one problem. He did not want to be alone in his last moments and he asked Marie if she was willing to be there as one of his closest friends. Not to help him end his life, but just to be there. Marie describes how on hearing this question her first reaction was one of anger and resistance. She was angry and somehow disappointed with him that he had asked her of all people. In the past years she had shared so much of her conversations with terminal patients with him that he should have known that life always opens up new doors when old doors are closed. Instead of responding to him by following her first impulses, however, she felt that there was another question behind his question. He was asking her if he could count on her as a friend, even in the hardest moments. He was appealing to her love for him, and suddenly she felt not only anger but also love inside her. She promised to be there, although she thought that his plan was absurd. Later in the book she describes how he had later come back to this earlier conversation. He told her that he saw things differently now. Her answer had created new space in his soul that enabled him to have confidence in the future again.

This story of Marie de Hennezel illustrates very well what is meant by the concept of inner space and why it is so central to the new *ars moriendi*. It is because of inner space that Marie was able to not react according to her first impulses. It helped her to sense various conflicting emotions, inner voices that dragged her in different directions. She was able to distinguish between the pain she felt herself by recording that the stories she had told were perhaps less well understood than she had always thought and the pain her friend must have because of his desperate plan. She was also able to find a balance and choose to respect the appeal that was made to her. And, most interestingly, it seemed as if her inner space was transferred to her friend by the way she responded to him. She describes that some months later his inner life had changed.

The interaction described here is similar to the one we saw in the preceding chapter. The way the nursing home physician responded to the woman in her mid-eighties who had filled in a euthanasia declaration was characterized by inner space and brought about the same in the old woman. And because of this quality, the fact that inner space helps to promote inner freedom in patients and those caring for them, the concept is of central importance to the new *ars moriendi*. In fact, the success of working with the model is dependent on the amount of inner space available.

In this chapter we will focus on two questions. The first is whether we can say something more about what inner space exactly is. Is it really something new or just old wine in new bottles? I will argue that what is new about inner space is not so much the phenomenon it appears to be, but rather the open way in which this phenomenon is conceptualized. The second question is very practical: How do we get there or foster it? As we will see, there are many roads that lead to Rome. In a sense, inner space is already there in a great number of things that are very familiar to us and are part of our everyday life. By identifying the dimension of inner space in them it might be easier to make them work for us when using the *ars moriendi* model.

Old wine in a new bottle?

Palliative care is an interdisciplinary approach to the pain and suffering caused by incurable diseases. The great thing about such an approach is that it has the explicit intention of looking at the entire person and his or her family system. It tries to avoid any reductionism that may be the result of focusing on merely the physical, psychological, social or spiritual dimension. In working in an interdisciplinary way, however, there are problems related to language and the way reality is framed. Every discipline has its own way of framing reality and ways of proceeding. In order to work with an interdisciplinary approach, one has to have a flexible mind.

The new *ars moriendi* and its central concept of inner space are developed as a way of integrating the spiritual dimension of care into this holistic approach. In order to do this, the model must add something to what is already being offered by other disciplines and should be open enough to be understood and integrated by people contributing from other disciplines. For this reason, the concept of inner space is deliberately presented and understood as a metaphor. In this way, the openness of the phenomenon it refers to is symbolically expressed in the status of the concept itself. The metaphor of inner space is composed of two spatial concepts and refers to a non-spatial phenomenon that can be perceived in an individual's inner life. If its metaphorical status is cherished, it is fit to function as an ambassador for the spiritual dimension and the centre of the new *ars moriendi* for a number of reasons.

First, inner space is a very simple concept that is easily recognized. People immediately understand that it is something they know very well from everyday life. It does not add something new that has to be learned, but something familiar that is reframed in such a way that it can be used for the benefit of ourselves and the people around us.

Second, inner space is a concept that is not limited to the mind or the body: it can be recognized in the corporeal experience of relief after roaring laughter or intense crying; it can be sensed in the emotional relief after a stressful event or period; and it can be experienced in the wonder or intellectual discovery of new perspectives. Inner space is not limited to those who can rationally and verbally express themselves but is also something that people suffering from dementia or intellectual disabilities may experience.

Third, inner space does not refer to specific emotions or ideals. It is not the same as inner peace or peace of mind as a state that all dying people should reach. Such ideals may add suffering when those who do not reach this state may feel they have failed even in their dying process. The openness of the metaphor honours the emotions and thoughts that are already there. It respects the inner polyphony of every human being without silencing one voice or the other for the sake of high ideals.

Fourth, inner space focuses on the process of communication and interaction that is central to the possibilities that may occur. The metaphor refers to a phenomenon that touches on both the inner lives and inner freedom of people, and the way these are mutually enriched and enlarged. Inner space refers to an inner process rather than a fixed state of mind. It is never finished or perfect but continuously changes, like the process of breathing in and breathing out.

Fifth, inner space is not limited to one specific discipline in palliative care. As a metaphor it is situated at the crossroads of spirituality, psychology, chaplaincy, ethics and social work. It is open to the dynamics that play a role in all these disciplines and can be translated and worked out in terms of the concepts and frameworks that are central to them.

Sixth, inner space is easily connected to the great spiritual traditions. It can be found in Christianity, Islam, Judaism, Hinduism, Buddhism and many more. It is not specifically limited to religious traditions, but rather refers to the elements in these traditions that are related to a shared anthropological background. This does not imply that it can be found everywhere to the same degree. Some spiritual traditions are more focused on inner space than others.

If inner space has all these qualities, and if the importance for the new *ars moriendi* cannot be underestimated, where then do we find it and how can we foster it in ourselves and in those we live with? We will now turn to that question. We will discuss six roads to inner space in order to make the phenomenon more accessible and concrete. These six roads form by no means an exhaustive list of possibilities, but will show a certain coherence as we proceed. We will begin with the road that is normally least associated with spirituality: humour.

Humour

People search for meaning. They do so in order to make sense of what is happening to them. Making sense of our existence is done by creating narratives in which we highlight specific things and leave other things out. We create narratives and narratives create us, as we will see in a later chapter. Narratives help us to find meaning and meaning brings orientation, stability and predictability by which we get the feeling of having control over our life. This is something we cannot do without, as we also saw in the first chapter where we touched on the existentialist analysis of fear and anxiety.

Meaning does help us to structure our world, but when this structure becomes too much a closed universe, another fundamental human need presents itself: the need for freedom. And there humour comes on the scene as a playful practice of creating free space in an unexpected way.

A couple of years ago one of my neighbours, a mother of three adolescents, told me she had been fretting a long time about doing something together with her children as a family again, just like in the old days when they were young and open to anything new. However, this is not an easy task with three adolescents each of whom have non-negotiable ideas about what is cool and what is uncool. After a long period of thought she came up with the idea of going to a concert of a band that was acceptable to all of them. Being proud of her achievement, and happy to be with her children at a special event, she drank a beer with her eldest son and said: 'This is something my parents never would have done, going to a pop concert with their children.' Her son looked up from his beer and dryly replied: 'Sure, but this is something you shouldn't do too often.'

This example can teach us a number of things about the relation between inner space and humour. In the first place it shows how humour opens up an unexpected new interpretation of the situation. The mother was clearly fishing for a compliment and hoped for a confirmation of her interpretation of the event. Her son put forward his interpretation. He seemed to express implicitly that it was very sweet of her to have organized this event, but that she should not forget that he also had his own life now. The surprise of this conflict of interpretations made her laugh.

The reaction of the mother, however, also tells us something else about humour. Any conflict of interpretations can lead to a struggle or a fight. There was a risk that the mother would not have been amused by this ungrateful response. She recognized the teasing tone of his answer and enjoyed the surprise of being confronted with her own one-sided perspective on the situation by someone who she knew did not want to hurt her. Humour always carries a risk with it – the risk of not being understood or being falsely interpreted. It presupposes some kind of connectedness and shared understanding that allows for the playfulness with interpretations without risking the relationship.

But humour also presupposes a willingness to let go of the interpretation one has a certain interest in. Humour is powerful and can be a threat for those whose power is dependent on a certain fixed way of looking at the world. Fanatics, fundamentalists and dictators are generally humourless (Oz 2010). They all feel threatened by anyone who plays with their interpretation of the world. They do not allow jokes about their way of seeing the world. They firmly hold on to a univocal interpretation of reality out of fear and lack of trust.

Humour is an important road to inner space. But it also has the capacity of opening up inner space in other people. When we laugh we physically experience inner space at an emotional level. When we tell a joke, our inner space spreads out to all who are laughing. This sharing of inner space highlights communality and creates community. In this sense the nature and prevalence of humour can also be a good indicator of the atmosphere in a team.

Humour, however, is no panacea. It only works when carefully adjusted to a situation and time. And humour isn't always funny either. Humour can be black, bitter, sceptical or cynical; it can hurt, offend and exclude people; it can be a ruthless weapon and a mean tactic. When, however, humour is used to build a life-sustaining web of relationships, it is a phenomenon that is closely related to spirituality because of its potential to open up new dimensions in and interpretations of reality.

The body

Palliative volunteers have played an important role in palliative care from its very beginning. Although volunteers are not formal caregivers and cannot do any medical or psychological intervention, their presence can be an important source of comfort and relief. I asked one of the volunteers what he valued about his work and he told me that he had the experience that his presence could really make a difference. I asked him for an example and he said that sometimes he stayed with a terminal patient during the night, sitting in a chair next to the bed.

During the night the patient sometimes became restless and uneasy. Often there was no possibility to talk with them because they would not respond. In those situations he would try to remain calm inside, be connected to himself and feel his inner space corporeally. In most of the cases it would seem as if this inner space was communicated to the patient, who also started to breathe more peacefully.

When I talked about this example during a lecture, a nurse said to me afterwards that she thought this wasn't anything special or unusual: when she was stressed, her dog became stressed as well. And when she was relaxed she would have a tranquillizing effect on her dog too. Of course she was right: as mammals we all share a dimension of corporeality that connects us. Some people can control horses, other people cannot. Dogs immediately sense it when you are afraid of them. We all remember from primary school that those teachers who did not have inner peace and connectedness with themselves were the ones that would have classes where it was extremely hard to keep order.

Our body is more than a vehicle to express what goes on in our mind, as we discovered in the first chapter in the work of Julia Lawton (1998, 2000). We have a body and we are our body (Merleau-Ponty 1945). Thus the way we are connected with our body is an important indicator of how we inhabit the world. In that sense, inner space concerns the complete mind-body unit that we human beings are. Our inner space is reflected in the way we behave. The body is the medium between the visible, material outer world and the invisible, emotional, mental, intellectual and spiritual inner world.

Inner space can be fostered by exercises like tai chi or yoga. It can be integrated in everyday caring practices by, for example, waiting a few seconds before entering a patient's bedroom, slowing down and connecting with the different time experience inside. And we know from communication science that the non-verbal bodily expressions, and the way we are located in the room, are an important part of what we transfer to others during conversations. We enlarge or shrink the inner space of the people we care for by the way we enter a room, greet someone or open the curtains. The calmness of our breathing, the sound of our voice, the look in our eyes, the quality of our touch all have impact on the inner space of ourselves, our colleagues and our patients.

The body is also the medium between the inner and outer space when it comes to the buildings in which we live and work. In recent years, hospital architecture has embraced the idea of the 'healing environment' in which the size of buildings, the proportions inside a room, the materials used, the colours and the light are all carefully thought about. Architecture is never neutral. Explicitly or implicitly, consciously or unconsciously it always reflects a view on the world and on life. Sometimes it is attuned to human beings, inviting, friendly and comforting. Sometimes it is meant to impress, to be functional or anonymous. The outer space is always connected to the inner space.

Emotions

Being confronted with death has an enormous impact on our emotional life, as we have seen in the first chapter. But how do we conceptualize the sensitivity of our inner life (Nussbaum 2001)? In everyday conversations we easily speak about emotions and feelings, using both as synonyms. In the scientific world there are many theories about emotions but there is no consensus on the definition.

There are many ways to make distinctions in the complex unity of corporeal and mental processes through which we interact with the world around us. In the majority of contemporary theories emotions are said to be composed of a number of elements: cognitive appraisal, bodily symptoms, action tendencies, expressions and feelings (Scherer 2005). The discussions are about the way these elements interact.

The concept of emotion has been used in scientific literature for the last three hundred years (Dixon 2003). Before that, the non-rational inner life was framed in terms of *passiones animae* or passions of the soul. The Latin word *passio* primarily refers to enduring or undergoing something. When it is something negative it can also refer to suffering, as in the passion of Christ, but the Latin connotation is broader than that. In English the Latin content of the word is still present in words like passive, patient and patience.

The old way of framing our emotional life expressed something very well that is less visible in contemporary theories of emotions: a sensitivity to the fact that human beings are not only actors but also receptive and vulnerable creatures that undergo a lot. The importance of this will be taken up later, when we come to speak about the question: 'How do I deal with suffering?' Its foundations, however, are directly connected to the concept of inner space.

During one of the coffee breaks at the palliative care unit where I did participatory observation research I expressed my admiration to the nursing staff that they were able to stay positive in their work and keep up a good mood amid all the pain and suffering they encounter. One of the nurses replied that they had a great team and their mutual support meant a lot to her, but she wouldn't want to think about how she would function in ten years.

She was afraid that someday she would pay the price for this emotional labour.

The term 'emotional labour' was coined by sociologist Arlie Hochschild in the 1980s and refers to the process of managing feelings and expressions in order to fulfil emotional requirements as part of a job role. Nurses are typical emotional workers that are constantly required to attune to a patient's mood and stay calm and friendly whatever happens. This demand may have an exhausting effect when the difference between what one feels and how one is supposed to behave is too great for a long period of time. Looking at emotions as something we undergo, we can imagine that there are limits to what people can endure.

Emotions can be an important road to inner space in that they tell us a lot about what we endure and what it does to us. In the old *passiones animae* tradition emotions were connected with spatial metaphors (Leget 2000). Fear, for example, is an emotion that reduces our inner space. When we are afraid of something we feel small and vulnerable. Physiological changes related to fear include the narrowing of our veins, which makes us look pale. Fear causes trembling legs, superficial breathing and a higher voice. It is as if we withdraw and are no longer able to be really connected with our body. The cognitive side of fear is also a narrowing of what we appreciate. We are so focused on the bad thing we feel threatened by that we lose every possibility of looking at things differently.

Love, however, is an emotion that enlarges our inner space. Love makes us feel large and strong, as if we could conquer the whole world. Our inner space seems to transcend the boundaries of our body and we seem to be able to connect with everything. Cognitively, love opens up an endless number of possible perspectives and possibilities. To love someone – and love is broader than romantic love, so this also goes for parental love and friendship – is to see a future for or with this person. To love someone is to share one's inner space with someone else.

Using emotions as a road to inner space helps us to stay in touch with our inner life and the resilience we have. This is important for working in healthcare – especially in palliative care – in order to stay healthy ourselves, and it is important in order to be able to open ourselves up for whatever patients have to tell us. Without inner space there will be no room inside for the things other people want to share with us.

Virtues

Emotions can be an important road to inner space because they tell us a lot about our inner life, and urge us to respect the capacity of our emotional life. They can also be a road to inner space in another sense: as a foundation for developing ourselves and creating more inner space by developing virtues.

The concept of virtue is as old as Western ethics. The idea that a morally good life is connected with the four cardinal virtues of justice, prudence, temperance and fortitude is already found in the works of Plato. Plato's pupil Aristotle worked it out further and made it the cornerstone of his ethics (Tongeren 2003). According to Aristotle, human beings are capable of leading a happy life by educating their emotional life. This is a lifelong process that is different for different people. Some people are born and raised in such a way that they will see dangers in everything they encounter. They develop an attitude of fear towards new experiences. Other people are born and raised in such a way that they never see any danger in what they encounter. They develop an attitude of recklessness. According to Aristotle, both will have to work on themselves to develop courage. The fearful person will have to expose himself to things he fears in order to discover that many times the fear is unjustified. The reckless person will have to experience that there really are dangerous situations in which one should be careful. Courage holds the middle position between fearfulness (no eye for danger) and recklessness (too much eye for danger). Courage can be developed by behaving courageously. It becomes a virtue when the right middle position is found easily, almost automatically as second nature, and one enjoys acting that way.

In what way can virtues become a road to inner space? In two ways, I think. First, acting virtuously is associated with acting easily and joyfully. For a virtuous person it costs no extra effort to be nice, empathetic, polite and just. He or she is just a nice, empathetic, polite and just person. From those long-term qualities, actions will flow that are likely to generate positive responses and confirm the attitude that is already there. Acting easily and joyfully one experiences inner space emotionally and cognitively. There is more room to invest in attention to what is needed here and now.

And second, the attitude of inner space itself can also be seen as a virtue that can be developed. Since all virtues are connected and have mutual impact on each other, the development of any one virtue may contribute to the development of any other virtue. Inner space may hold a position similar to that of prudence – the ability to make the right decision in whatever specific situation – in classical and medieval philosophy. In the work of Thomas Aquinas, for example, prudence is seen as the virtue that directs all other virtues and is perfectly integrated in the virtuous person. Likewise inner space, as second nature, enables us to endure and live with the many voices in ourselves and could be seen as an attitude that has great impact on the kind of personality we are.

Speaking about virtues is not common in healthcare. We live in an age in which practices are more and more regulated by guidelines, requirements and protocols. And when we reflect on the abilities of those who work in healthcare we tend to speak about competencies rather than virtues. In designing a new *ars moriendi,* we must consider how detailed such a model should be and in what direction it should be developed. There are three reasons why it is important to be careful in developing a contemporary *ars moriendi* as a strict protocol.

In the first place, working according to guidelines and protocols has the danger of a tick-box approach. As long as everything is done according to the external requirements, the process and its outcome should be good. Every art, however – and the *ars moriendi* is no exception – is based on acquiring capacities in practice that come from the inside. Such capacities become second nature, just like the virtues. Inner space cannot be learned from a book. Not even this one. It can only be experienced and practised in real life.

In the second place, working according to guidelines and protocols is based on the idea that without them things go terribly wrong. But where people have a logic of fear and distrust they enter an endless spiral of checking and controlling that will never be enough. The care for vulnerable people, however, is only possible in a culture of trust. Only in such a culture can inner space be found and fostered.

In the third place, working according to guidelines and protocols is based on what can be measured. But trying to measure inner space and virtues is missing the point. Competencies can be measured by their effect. Inner space and virtues are on a different road towards what is good. Here it is not just the effect that counts; their value and goodness lie in every moment of the process itself. Inner space and virtues are not instrumental qualities but already participate in the process of living and dying well they seek to realize.

This having been said, we should not be naive or romantic. The world we live in needs guidelines and protocols because of the great complexity and overdose of information we have to deal with. And guidelines are not principally opposed to spirituality, as we have known ever since Moses came down from Mount Sinai with the Ten Commandments. Perhaps also here we should prudently search for a middle position that is characteristic of a virtuous life.

Spiritual traditions

Many spiritual traditions offer ways of discovering and fostering inner space. For example, in the Christian tradition, stories function as a way of opening up a different perspective on the world. Like humour, the stories are part of an alternative view on reality – a world in which unique events and experiences that are beyond our imagination decide which way to go, not statistics and majorities.

Visiting one of the great medieval cathedrals, one enters a micro cosmos, a little universe in itself. Standing in the middle of the church and looking at the sun making visible the images of saints shining in the stained glass windows, one might suddenly experience being surrounded by fellow travellers on the same road from many ages before. Religion can redefine our place in life and our identity by the way it invites us to become part of a larger story with greater ambitions than any individual can dream of. As part of a religious or spiritual tradition one can discover inner space by hearing that one is a child of God or on the path to enlightenment. In one of the later chapters we will show how the *ars moriendi* model can be used in a religious context.

Because religious and spiritual traditions can have the power of redefining the way we appreciate reality, they have an inherent danger of becoming a goal in itself, diverting us from the invisible reality that is their core business – *per visibilia ad invisibilia*, through the visible to the invisible, as the famous medieval saying goes. In most religious and spiritual traditions, therefore, we see also movements of purification and self-correction. According the Ten Commandments, it is forbidden to make an image of God, and Islam holds a similar view. Both in the mystical traditions and in the works of the great theologians there is a deep awareness that God is incomprehensible and beyond the power of human intellect.

One of the most successful movements that has been integrated into the healthcare sector in recent years is mindfulness. That mindfulness has found such a great resonance in the contemporary world is partly due to the work of the Vietnamese monk and peace activist Thich Nhat Hanh (1975) but it is thanks to the work of the American molecular biologist Jon Kabat-Zinn that the concept was accepted in the world of science and medicine.

Mindfulness can be described as mild open attentiveness. It is a practice of unprejudiced and open acceptance of what is there: inside you and in your environment. Mindfulness can be seen as a very concrete and practical exercise in achieving what is meant by the metaphor of inner space. It focuses on living in the here and now, becoming aware of the polyphony inside oneself and not judging or suppressing the many voices one discovers. We do not coincide with what we think. We cannot be reduced to what we think. Our mind is only part of what we are. There is always more.

Silence

'When my 19-year-old son suddenly died,' a mother told me, 'there was nothing left of me but sadness and anger. Many people did not know how to respond to the situation and did not have the courage to visit us. One person who did come was our GP. He expressed how sorry he was and he sat down in a chair. He just sat there, without saying anything. I went to the kitchen to make him a coffee, but at a certain moment I couldn't help but burst out to him, saying: "You just sit there, saying nothing." He looked at me and said: "I am so terribly sorry about what has happened to you. I do not know what to say." At that time I did not realize how important this moment was. Looking back, however, I discovered that it brought me so much comfort that he had come. I am still grateful to him for this.'

Silence comes in many ways. There is the silence of an early Sunday morning when the whole world is quiet and serene; the silence of the night when traffic has come to rest; the silence of a long hot summer afternoon in July; the silence of a crystal clear February morning when the world is covered in white snow; the silence high up in the mountains; the silence in a concert hall after the final chord has been played; the silence in a church during prayer. But there is also the silence of someone who doesn't know how to respond; the silence of someone whose voice is not heard; the silence of someone who is ashamed; the silence before the storm; the silence before hell breaks loose in a fight; the silence after a last scream of suffering; the silence of people who know each other so well that words are not needed; the silence in a real conversation; the silence of people who are reading for themselves in the same room; the silence during Remembrance Day.

Silence as a road to inner space is the silence that connects us with our deepest thoughts and feelings. All great pieces of literature, poetry, philosophy and music are born out of silence. Beethoven and Nietzsche spent their mornings taking walks for hours, during which they developed ideas in silence. In the afternoon these ideas would be written down and worked out. Silence plays a major role in spiritual traditions. Meditation is built on silence. Churches, cloisters and abbeys are traditionally places of silence. Silence can be healing and comforting. But silence may also take courage.

A retired professor of nursing home medicine told me that he used to give all medical students who did an internship with him the same assignment: to enter the room of a patient who suffered from an incurable disease, sit down and just see what happens. He knew from experience that young doctors are inclined to walk past those patients since they have the idea they cannot offer anything meaningful. Moreover, they are afraid of the silence in those rooms. From time to time, after many years he would meet these younger colleagues again and they all told him the same: they could hardly remember what they had learned during their internship, but these moments in silence had made a huge impression on them.

Silence can be confronting. Many people do not like to be alone with it. They only feel comfortable after they have turned on the television or radio. Silence can be trained and, in fact, many of the roads to inner space discussed in this chapter can be roads to silence: experiencing one's body, becoming aware of one's emotions, the many practices that have been developed in religious and spiritual traditions: all of them are roads to silence or ways of doing something that require silence.

With silence as the last of the roads to inner space we come to the end of this chapter. Now we have an overview of the *ars moriendi* model, the nature and importance of inner space and the many roads to get there, in the following five chapters we will focus on the five central themes in more detail. In accordance with the great importance that is attributed to autonomy in contemporary healthcare we will start with the question: 'Who am I and what do I really want?'

Who Am I and What Do I Really Want?

O ne of the patients I was involved in taking care of in the nursing home was an older man who had had a stroke and could move only half of his body. The nurses thought I would want to meet him. When I asked them why they thought so, there came no clear answer. I thought I saw some inner naughtiness in their eyes, so I was curious to learn more of this man. As I approached him he greeted me with great enthusiasm and I introduced myself. He immediately asked me about my last name. He supposed this name must be French and he guessed my ancestors must have been Huguenots, just like his forefathers. I confirmed his guess and told him that our family tree had been traced back to the early seventeenth century when one of my forefathers had fled from the south of France to the Netherlands. As our conversation continued I was impressed by how well educated this man was and how broad his interest in the world. At the same time, I had a somewhat curious feeling about the way the conversation developed. On the one hand, he seemed to seek similarities between the two of us; he had also done very well in school and had enjoyed a university education. On the other hand, by doing so he seemed to single out the two of us from the rest of the people working in the nursing home. Moreover, I noticed that it was always him who was posing the questions and always me who was answering. More and more the conversation began to feel like an interrogation during a job interview. I decided to turn the tables and began to ask him about his life story. He turned out to have been born in Indonesia, a former Dutch colony, and had led an interesting and rich life. After his graduation at university he had made a career in the banking world but many things had gone wrong in a short time. And now he had ended up in a four-bed room in a nursing home. He clearly did not feel comfortable here and could not adjust to his new home. He behaved like a bank director, summoned personnel and gave orders, but did not manage to make friends or to gain sympathy with the nursing staff. He felt that his life was no longer worth living. He did not know why he would want to go on anymore. He was frustrated that although he was a competent patient, no one would help him to end his life. During the coffee break the nurses wanted to know how it had gone with the older man. I realized that I was torn between different feelings. I felt sorry for this man who seemed to be trapped in a self-inflicted loneliness. But I could also understand why he was the most unpopular patient on the ward. What puzzled me more, however, was who this man really was. According to Dutch law he might be regarded as a competent patient whose autonomy should be respected, but to what extent could he be regarded as someone capable of free choice?

A society of autonomous individuals

Respect for the autonomy of patients is an important correction in northern European and North American bioethics and law to a long tradition of medical paternalism. Patients who have the mental capacities to make a realistic estimation of their interests should be able to decide about their treatment. In most countries this means that if patients do not wish to be treated any longer, they may refuse further treatment, even if this will mean that it may lead to their death. Of course, this should be documented well so that there is no doubt about pressure from others (such as family members who are waiting for an inheritance) and it should be the free will of the individual.

In some countries or states it is possible to ask for assisted dying or euthanasia. In that case again there are procedures and regulations in order to warrant the patient's capacity and exclude any external pressure. Basically, however, the patient is seen as an individual who is in charge of his or her own life, and the general feeling seems to be that practices in which others determine whether a person lives or dies should be reduced to a minimum.

This culture of self-determination that has developed in the last thirty years has been paralleled with and fostered by the rise of neoliberalism (Brown 2003). According to this ideology, individual freedom is seen as the most important social value, and this freedom should be attained by minimal state functions. At the same time, market values are disseminated to social politics and to all institutions. An economic rationale pervades our thinking. As a result of this, individuals are more and more seen as entrepreneurs who have to give shape to their own individual existence and are responsible for their own lives. People should always be highly performing and calculating in order to be successful, and this success is equalled to happiness.

Neoliberal thinking has a great impact on the way we organize society and look at ourselves. One of its effects is that caring, a practice that is essential to the coherence of a society, is radically transformed (Brugère 2014). From a relational practice, a kind of engagement that constitutes community and is shared spontaneously between people living close to each other, care becomes first and foremost an individual responsibility toward oneself. As with all other activities that come under an economic rationale, care is seen as an activity where human beings deploy their human capital. According to the market, human capital must bear fruit, so caring becomes seen as the investment and production of human capital.

According to this neoliberalist ideology, human beings are seen as autonomous and self-reliant. Dependency and vulnerability are seen as a weakness or defect. These defects create a market for those who are fit enough to be carers. These caring activities are seen as economic exchanges. Those who are not able to participate in the economic exchange but do so as consumers are clearly falling short of the ideal and norm of a strong, self-reliant individual.

The idea of freedom associated with neoliberalism is a form of negative freedom: it is not defined by any positive content. This kind of freedom is defined by the absence of interference. Of course, the picture we just painted can be expounded by distinguishing many different cultures in both Europe and the United States where people are less seen as autonomous individuals and more as members of a family. In the Mediterranean countries, for example, traditionally there are different views about the relation between the individual and the family he or she belongs to. But also in these cultures the impact of neoliberalism is felt and also here we see changes over time.

When we look at the older man in the nursing home through the lens of the neoliberalist view of individual autonomy, it is rather easy to find an answer to the questions that puzzled me. Whoever this man was is not of any importance. We do not need to know. And the question of whether he is a free man or not is easily settled by looking at his intellectual performance. Since he is a competent adult, of importance is how he can be helped to fulfil his wishes and end his life. Neoliberalism does not need an *ars moriendi*. Dying is seen as a private matter, an individual affair. The question, however, is whether this way of looking at the end of life does not do great injustice to people. Forgetting that people are not only individuals but also social beings, not only self-reliant entrepreneurs but also vulnerable and dependent beings, is denying half of what people in the end are.

Reflecting on the situation of the dying in the early 1980s, Norbert Elias concluded that dying people are left alone in many ways (Elias 1985). One of these ways is the idea that they have to find a meaning in life all by themselves. Individualism has pervaded so deeply our contemporary culture that we think that our life can have an individual meaning apart from the meaning it has to other people. If we do not find this meaning we are disappointed and call life meaningless. The strange thing is that as long as we just live and act we are experiencing the interrelatedness of meaning and connectedness all the time, but as soon as we start to reflect on our life we make this mistake.

If we do not want to leave the older man alone in his despair and isolation, we might want to reflect a little further on his so-called autonomy. If autonomy is composed of the words 'self' and 'determination', the question of who this man is might be an important lead to understanding his situation. Our new *ars moriendi* should be able to help us here.

Myself and the other

Mentally competent people sometimes surprise both themselves and others. Marie de Hennezel's friend who wanted to end his life at the age of 65 had reflected long on his decision. Subsequently he took the courage to share his decision with one of his best female friends. The woman listened to him, did not try to make him change his mind but confirmed that she would be there for him, and after a couple of months he reported that he had come back to his decision. The fact that she had listened to him with open attention and had not judged him had helped him to develop a new perspective on his life.

Human freedom is not always easy to determine, and considering the tricks that death plays on us, we might suspect that Marie de Hennezel's friend had been driven by fear or anxiety. In order to respect a patient's autonomy it might, therefore, not be sufficient to just write down what a patient has to say. If we want to respect a person as a human being, it is perhaps the inner conversation of the patient that deserves our attention. But if the patient has an inner conversation, which of these inner voices represent the real self? Or is there not one voice representing the real self but rather a singing choir representing different inner voices that seek harmony?

In his later works the French philosopher Paul Ricoeur has reflected on the nature of the human self on the crossroads of linguistics, narrative theory, ethics and ontology (Ricoeur 1990). According to his analysis, which is one of the theoretical cornerstones of our *ars moriendi*, he discerns three relations that together constitute the 'self' as an ongoing process in time. Let us take a look at the older man in the nursing home and ask ourselves the question: Who is he?

A first way to answer this question is to describe him as someone who has great difficulty in presenting a coherent life story, or rather difficulty in identifying with a broken life story. He does not feel at home in the nursing home and keeps on sending signals that he is not the person he seems to be. He is not the vulnerable non self-reliant individual one sees when looking at him. He is an important man who has been stranded in the wrong place after the winds of fate have blown his ship in the wrong direction.

A second way to answer this question is to describe the old man simply as a lonely man who has great problems building good relationships with the people he shares his everyday life with. He isolates himself by communicating in a manner that is not adjusted to the situation. He fails to be connected with the people around him and seems not to be sure of who he is.

A third way to describe him is as a former bank director who has ended up as a severe stroke patient in a nursing home.

Each one of these three ways of describing the older man is correct, they all bring a different constituting relationship to the fore, and they are all interrelated. Describing him as someone who has difficulty in identifying with his life story (the relation between me and myself), is expressed in the fact that he does not know how to relate with the people around him (the relation between myself and the others), which is based on the fact that he has always identified himself with the position he had in society (the relation between myself and the institutions).

If we situate these three self-constituting relationships with regard to the poles of 'oneself' and 'the others', the first relationship (between me and myself) is on the 'oneself' side of the spectrum, and the other two relationships (between myself and the others, and myself and the institutions – or myself and the others through the institutional dimension) are on the other side of the spectrum. Both ends of the spectrum need each other. We are not entirely self-made or able to define ourselves by ourselves alone: we did not invent the language which enables us to think and express ourselves in the first place, let alone the fact that we wouldn't even survive if we had not been taken care of during the first years of our lives by other people who, in most cases, also provided our DNA. However, we are not just the products of our environment, education and culture; most of us are unique, free, responsible and creative human beings capable of influencing who and what we are by the choices that we make.

Understanding the self as a continuous dialectical process between two poles has a great impact on how we see autonomy. It means that we cannot consider autonomy as the result of the relation between me and myself alone. From the outset the relation between myself and the others, and the institutional context of this, plays a major role. Let us, before turning to the role of inner space in this process, turn shortly to the three relationships that constitute the self in order to see more clearly the contribution and importance of each of them.

The relation between me and myself is mediated by language and storytelling. Even the relation with our emotions and feelings is mediated by the framework in which we experience them. The pain I experience visiting a dentist will be completely different from the moment I am no longer sure that the dentist is filling a hole in my tooth or a hole in his bank account. Living is interpreting and this also goes for the way in which I see myself. Our life story is a continuous creative process in which single actions and practices become meaningful in the light of larger life goals. Similar to the way we understand a book by a dialectical hermeneutical process between the parts and the whole (words have meaning in sentences, sentences in paragraphs, and so on), we understand ourselves in a dialectal process. By understanding ourselves we compose an image of who we are by selecting and combining ways of looking on ourselves. Every life story can be told in a million different ways and we will have conscious or subconscious reasons for choosing to tell it one way or the other.

From the outset our own life story is part of the life stories of many other people. Their stories have an impact on the way we see ourselves as well. A married person may have a great sense of responsibility for the happiness of his or her spouse and children. This responsibility may fortify inner voices that frame one's identity in terms of being a wife and mother of children first and foremost, as opposed to being also an employee and attractive colleague open to exciting love affairs. But suddenly one may discover oneself to be so deeply in love that a crisis of identity may come about. People may discover they do things they would never have thought of themselves. Our actions correct the image we have formed of ourselves.

The voices of other people telling us who and what we are is not limited to those who are alive; in many people's lives those who have passed away play a continuing role, sometimes consciously through inner conversations ('How proud my father would have been if he had known...'), sometimes unconsciously through the bonds of loyalties. In both cases, however, our identity is so much interwoven with that of other people that it might sometimes seem that we are nothing more than the sum of our relationships with other people. Human life is always embedded in larger structures, transcending the interpersonal dimension. Institutions like healthcare, justice, education, church, or state all play their role in defining who we are, how we see ourselves, how we look at other people and what our chances in life are. The older man defined his identity institutionally in terms of being a bank director. He could not live with the new institutional identity imposed on him, that of a nursing home patient. In his view, from the camp of the winners he was unwillingly transported to the camp of the losers, and he refused to take up that new identity.

Institutions are important to guarantee permanency and stability in societies, although in the last decades we see that institutions seem to be under more and more pressure (Dubet 2002). But even if institutions change and develop into new forms, they continue to play an important role in stabilizing human relations. The downside of institutions, however, is that they are blind and can become rigid and bureaucratic. Institutions can be dehumanizing and detrimental to the self-esteem of people. Any *ars moriendi* that is not naive should be alert to this negative side effect.

Inner space

If our self is constituted in a dialectical process between the two poles of me and myself on the one hand, and me and the others on the other hand, what does this then mean for our understanding of autonomy? And what is the role of inner space in this process? As we have seen in the preceding chapter, inner space enables one to be open to discovering polyphony inside oneself. The more inner space there is, the more one is able to acknowledge that there might be a number of voices inside oneself that ask to be heard. All of these voices are situated somewhere on the continuum between the me-pole and the other-pole between which the dialectical process takes place. Having inner space means being able to hear those inner voices without feeling any urgency to resolve the tension that might occur when these voices are not in harmony with each other.

If we reflect on the story of Marie de Hennezel again and ask ourselves if her reaction was a free autonomous reaction to her friend, we have an illustration of this process. On hearing his request for her to be there when he ended his life, the first things she felt were anger, resistance and disappointment. These emotions were directly connected to the me-pole of her identity. Because he asked her to be present at this moment she felt denied of how she saw herself – a women who was dedicated to discovering the quality of life and new perspectives in her daily work with dying people. But because she had inner space, she also felt emotions that were connected with the other-pole of her identity, emotions connected with their long-lasting and special friendship that meant a lot to her. She was able to perceive the importance of conflicting perspectives inside herself that were both deeply rooted in who she was. At the same time, she sensed that at this moment for this man it was important to give priority to the appeal that was made on their friendship. But she formulated her answer in such a way that she neither had to betray the me-pole nor the other-pole in herself. She said she would be there, although she did not support his absurd idea.

Marie de Hennezel's story is an example of inner freedom and autonomy. She retained freedom with regard to her emotions; although she did perceive them, she was not bound or forced by any of them. She did not suppress or deny any single one of her conflicting emotions, but took the time to investigate what they were telling her about the situation she was in. Moreover, she was able to make a judgement about the weight of both conflicting perspectives. Both poles, both perspectives had their own value, and she felt that both were connected to who she was.

If inner space helps to bear or even integrate emotions that are related to conflicting poles, what then happens when there is no inner space? Reconsidering the situation of the older man in the nursing home may help us here. This man seemed to have a clear idea of what he wanted: he did not want to live anymore. When we analyse his death wish we see that it was another way of saying that he did not want to live in that situation according to those conditions. In his case there was also a conflict between how he saw himself and how his situation in real life was. From the way he told his life story and the way he communicated with the people around him it was clear that he defined his identity by his institutional position. Being a bank director was more than his job. It was how he saw himself and how he wanted to be seen by others. By defining his identity via the other-pole, he took a great risk because when he moved to a nursing home as a patient, he did not know how to integrate this new situation into his life story. Being vulnerable, dependent and partly paralysed were parts of his life story that were denied and kept out of sight. He did not have the inner space to reconcile the different emotions and perspectives that were related to his identity, and instead chose to step out of life rather than to confront and endure this situation.

Does this mean that Marie de Hennezel's reaction was better than the reaction of the older man? Is the new *ars moriendi* perhaps more moralistic than we want to admit? The new *ars moriendi* is not meant to judge people or to push them in a certain direction. It is meant to help people to discover an inner freedom that enables them to reconcile with themselves and the people around them. In this sense it is not morally neutral. In the background there is a normative position of seeing society as a life-sustaining web of relationships rather than a free market where the sky is the limit. And comparing Marie de Hennezel with the older man, there seems to be little doubt that she has more inner space and her autonomous choice is more characterized by inner freedom.

The case of dignity

Situations involving end-of-life discussions like the one in which the older man found himself are often framed as situations where human dignity is threatened. What is life worth when people are no longer able to relate to their actual situation and they have lost their self-esteem? If people feel that the life they are leading is no longer worth living, are we then not obliged to help them die out of respect for their sense of dignity? If people wish to preserve the image of who they once were, for the sake of their dignity, who are we to deny them of this?

Discussions on human dignity have a tendency to become very confusing, for dignity is a concept carrying more than two thousand years of connotations from a great variety of cultural contexts (Kirchhoffer 2013). In my view, in the current discussions where this concept plays a role there are three ways in which the word is used, related to three different meanings (Leget 2013b).

Sometimes dignity is seen as the way it is defined in the Universal Declaration of Human Rights, where it is said that dignity is inherent to being born as a human being. This interpretation follows an old tradition, already present in Stoic thinking and developed in Christian theology, where dignity is something intrinsically connected with being human. Human dignity is an ontological category: it can be threatened, denied or harmed but cannot be lost. It applies to all creatures that are born from human parents, however vulnerable or disabled. This meaning of the word can be connected with the institutional dimensions of identity, since it is not visible or tangible, but proclaimed by institutions like the United Nations and the Church.

A second way in which the word is used is in relation to other people. In the oldest meaning of the word, dignity was something which was bestowed on certain people who held public offices. Dignity in this sense can be lost and is dependent on the way people treat each other. This sense of dignity can be recognized in both social and interpersonal relations. Treating someone with respect is honouring his or her dignity. People can be treated in a way that takes away their dignity or establishes their dignity. This meaning of the word can be connected with the interpersonal dimension of identity.

The third way in which the concept is used is relatively new and often found in end-of-life discussions. Here the word is used as a subjective category referring to the self-esteem people experience. People can be in a situation where they feel they lose their self-esteem because they can no longer identify with the kind of person they have become in their own eyes. This use of the term can refer to a great variety of situations. For some people this occurs when they are no longer able to control their bowels (think of the case of Annie that Julia Lawton described), for others it is connected to suffering from dementia, and some people connect it with no longer having a goal in life. In all these cases the sensed loss of dignity is related to a loss of freedom. And here we find the connection to autonomy and the reason why the two concepts are so often used simultaneously or even synonymously. In the case of the older man in the nursing home, we see that the term is used in the third sense. He obviously does not see any more purpose in life, having lost his self-esteem and being unable to adapt to the new life situation. Does that mean that we are in a dead-end street here? If he has lost his self-esteem and utters an autonomous wish to die, how can any new *ars moriendi* then be of use?

Autonomy, dignity and the art of dying

The three meanings of dignity, just like the three relations constituting the self, are related to each other and are mutually interacting in a dialectical process. In the end, interpersonal dignity is the fundamental one. With regard to ontological dignity it is clear that this does not really mean anything in terms of having an impact on reality, unless it is put into practice among human beings. Proclaiming that women have the same dignity as men, but denying them the same rights and freedom simultaneously, is nothing more than proclaiming a lie.

But also subjective dignity is dependent on the practices of interpersonal dignity. Self-esteem is generated and built up in interactions with other people in which one is confirmed as being special as a human being. There is a lot of research in developmental psychology confirming this. Therefore, healthcare institutions proclaiming the importance of dignity should invest in creating an atmosphere in which interpersonal dignity is fostered and lived.

If we apply this to the older man in the nursing home, we could say that confirming his perceived lack of self-esteem is leaving him alone and in the end quite literally killing him. Denying his sensed lack of self-esteem and proclaiming ontological dignity is hardly any better, since also then the man is left to his own devices. In the new *ars moriendi* the middle way of interpersonal dignity is the royal road along which we can try to foster his autonomy by trying to foster his inner space. What could this look like?

The Canadian psychiatrist and palliative care physician Harvey Chochinov has developed a 'dignity therapy' intervention that aligns very well with this part of the *ars moriendi* model as we have developed it (Chochinov 2002, Chochinov *et al.* 2005). In this model the patient is asked to tell his life story and remember the good things of life. In this way the patient is given the opportunity to reframe his or her situation from the perspective of having had a life worth living. Being invited by someone who listens attentively has a comforting and even healing effect. The act of really listening to someone is an act of bestowing interpersonal or social dignity on them. Inner space plays a central role here.

For the one listening, inner space allows them to be really present, taking time, having attention, without any other goal in mind. In the comforting presence of someone really listening, a patient is given the opportunity to open up and discover new dimensions to their life story. Telling one's life story is a creative act. In this creative act unexpected new connections can be discovered and the image of oneself can be retrieved. A reappraisal of oneself involves a reappraisal of one's situation and future.

If I were to enter into a conversation with the older man in the nursing home and listen to the many voices in the way he told his life story, a new perspective on who he was might be opened. Valuable aspects of himself that he had silenced or neglected might be remembered and given voice. The inner space that could be developed in that way would foster his inner freedom and autonomy. His wish to die might remain – there would be no guarantee that this would change – but the anger and frustration from which it was born might be taken away. He might still define his identity by the important role in society he has played. But if it was done out of inner space, the way he is connected to himself and the people around him would be completely different. He would no longer cling to his former role as a shipwrecked person clings to a piece of wood, but feel connected to his rich past in a way that would give him peace of mind. In the *ars moriendi* model it is not being more connected to one pole or the other which is right or wrong, but the way in which one relates to the poles. The more inner space one has, the more autonomy and dignity will be experienced. The more inner space one has, the more inner freedom and authenticity one may develop.

5

How Do I Deal
with Suffering?

The first time I saw Mr McNeal he was sitting in a chair opposite the reception desk in the nursing home, waiting to be brought to the palliative care unit. Like a helpless, skinny bird, he looked around him with his coat on, a cap on his head, surrounded by oxygen bottles. Most striking were his huge ears. Mr McNeal had been a sailor most of his life. Almost 80 years old, he had been around the world seven times. He had been married for many years, but his wife had died some years ago. The couple had never had children. And now it suddenly seemed all over. He had been diagnosed with lung cancer. The GP had said he thought Mr McNeal would not make it longer than a week or two.

As he entered his new room, he was completely out of breath. First he needed to sit down. A cup of coffee, a roll-up cigarette. His cap on the table. A bald, tanned head. Big hands. Lively eyes. When his bags and oxygen bottles were brought in, one of the physicians entered the room for an introductory consultation. Mr McNeal had brought quite a pharmacy with him. The bed was covered with medication bottles and boxes.

'You know doctor, I am not ill.'

'You are ill, I'm afraid.'

'But I don't feel ill.'

'Okay.'

Boundaries were being explored and tested. Fears shimmered through. He was afraid to be out of breath, to suffocate. But he was also afraid that they would give him an injection, although he was in possession of a euthanasia declaration. Moreover, he was determined to still be around for the world championship football during the coming summer. He had placed a bet about it with his GP.

A pro-active society

Never before in human history has medicine been able to keep us alive for so long. People live longer in good health in the North Atlantic world, and babies born in the year 2000 are expected to have a life expectancy of one hundred years. Growing old in good health is an important goal for many people, and the healthcare sectors in the world's richest countries consume so much money that they all struggle to keep the costs down.

We live in an age in which we – more than any generation before us – harvest the fruits that have been sown many centuries ago. From the sixteenth century when Andreas Vesalius mapped out human anatomy and the seventeenth century when William Harvey discovered the circulation of the blood, medical science has developed steadily. In the eighteenth century the conviction was born that one day all diseases would be cured and death would be banned. After the Second World War medical developments gained momentum in a spectacular way, paralleled by many other technological developments that have fundamentally changed our way of living and dying.

As a result of these developments the dying process has become medicalized – death is seen as a medical problem that should be dealt with from a medical perspective first and foremost. Leaving the dying process in the hands of the doctors has brought us a lot: people live longer, die with less pain, are better supported in all dimensions and all this is monitored, measured and documented with the help of a great number of reliable scales and instruments. But there are also a number of side effects that give new food for thought.

As we saw before in the first chapter of this book, by framing the dying process as a medical process we tend to convince ourselves that we are safe. Death is something for old age, and we can be sure that we do not have to worry in the safe hands of skilled physicians and nurses. We tend to forget that even in the North Atlantic world many people still die from poverty, traffic accidents, natural disasters, murders, suicides and terrorist attacks (Kellehear 2016).

From a medical perspective, the most important consequence is that human action in end-of-life matters becomes part of an instrumental rationality with its own logic and dynamism. This has great impact on our freedom of choice. At first sight, it would seem that the development of medical technology has multiplied our options and freedom of choice. Paradoxically, however, we are not free, but forced to choose among more and more options. This might seem great for people who like to be in control over their living and dying, but not all people are like that. Many patients do not want to be confronted with complex choices of which they cannot oversee the consequences. They just want to entrust themselves to the caring hands of others.

Also, when we are confronted with choices, there is a strong tendency to act and perform rather than to abstain. This tendency is shared among physicians, patients and relatives, who hold each other in a grip that only reinforces this tendency. Let us take a closer look at how this works.

Physicians are trained in doing, searching for solutions, trying and not giving up. This is shown in the way medical curricula are set up, but it is also expected from their patients. Having visited their GP, patients would rather go home with pills that might not be effective than hear that they should just wait and see for a couple of days. Doing nothing is connected with feelings of guilt and (anticipated) remorse. Doing things is connected with feeling good, heroism and gratefulness. The most prestigious and well-paid parts of medicine are connected with heroic operations on vital organs, not taking care of disabled, older or dying patients.

Patients want to survive as long as possible. They are inclined to take every chance, however small, for recovery, survival or postponement of death. This is a natural instinct in virtually every human being who is not suffering from a severe psychiatric disease. Moreover, often there is an urge to try every possible option so that one might not feel regret or guilt at not having tried everything possible. People tend to regret what they have not done more than what they have actually done, which also inclines one to take action rather than do nothing.

Relatives often have strong motives to urge patients and physicians to try every possible option, either because they are not ready to say goodbye and need more time, or they feel guilty for not wanting the patient to be alive as long as possible. Since all tendencies of these three groups point in the same direction, it is clear that when they come together a strong preference for action is shared by all.

This tendency towards action causes a range of new problems. Next to the fear of being undertreated and dying too early, in many societies a new problem presents itself. Many people are afraid to die from diseases that occur relatively often at an older age, such as Alzheimer's or Parkinson's disease. As long as there is no cure for these diseases many older people are confronted with the issue of how to avoid this situation. And apart from this there seems to be a growing number of older people who consider their lives no longer worth living, because they live in a tangle of unwillingness and inability to connect with what their life has become (Wijngaarden, Leget and Goosensen 2016).

This situation then causes an excess of responsibilities. Because everything is transposed in the key of action, and all actions can be connected to responsibilities, there seem to be no choices left for which there is no direct or indirect medical responsibility. If a patient lives the doctor is responsible, if the patient dies the doctor is responsible as well. And since responsibility is an ethical category, there seems no way to look at something as just happening without anyone to blame for it.

And finally, although everything is seen as part of human responsibility and connected with choices that have been made, the medical domain itself – purely instrumental as its rationality is – does not offer any orientation in the choices that need to be made. Medical doctors are expected to be able to interpret statistics and calculate probable effects and outcomes. Which of these effects and outcomes are desired by the patient, however, can only be decided by the patient. Nevertheless, many patients expect the physicians to help them make up their minds when confronted with something as frightening as death playing tricks on them.

The predilection to doing rather than abstaining is not limited to medicine. It is reflected in many other areas in our culture and fostered by a neoliberal climate in which all citizens are supposed to be entrepreneurs. If we accept the blessings of contemporary medicine and acknowledge that we cannot step outside the culture we live in, what corrections then are possible in this logic and what can be expected from a new *ars moriendi*?

Doing and undergoing

With regard to autonomy, we have seen that the new *ars moriendi* opens up the idea of an isolated individuals who have to choose on their own. Approaching the self as relational helps to develop an idea of autonomy that is open to the polyphony inside us. Between the inner poles of me and the others, the self can develop inner space and a more free and open attitude, allowing people to make decisions together at the end of life.

With regard to human action and the way we deal with suffering a similar idea is proposed. By reframing the idea of human action in a dialectical polarity of doing and undergoing, we create a broader spectrum of possibilities that are closer to real life. With this correction on an over-activist approach to human action we align with the thought of great philosophers like Thomas Aquinas and Paul Ricoeur, who developed the idea that in the interaction with their environment human beings both perform and undergo things.

Doing and undergoing can be approached as two poles in a dialectical process and they can be seen as opposites – and in fact they often are – but as we will see there are many examples of human practices where they are integrated. Let us start by looking at them as opposites, then connect them with inner space and finally look at two examples of practices where they are integrated.

People who are confronted with a life-terminating illness may react in opposite ways. There are people who immediately start to arrange things. They prepare for the worst by being in control of everything and being sure that nothing happens that they do not agree with. They start to write a living will or – as it happens in my own country – a euthanasia declaration; they start to think about their possessions, the things they would like to do and the people they would like to see, and some people even prepare their funeral in all its detail.

Others react in completely the opposite way. They do not prepare for the worst or for anything else and just keep on living as they always have. It seems as if nothing has happened, and their life simply goes on. They might even continue to go to their work, planning their holiday in six months' time, living life as any other person without a life-threatening disease would do.

Reading these two examples one might easily be tempted to call the first person a control freak and the second person someone who is in a phase of denial. The question, however, is whether one can say anything reasonable about these two people without knowing anything about the inner space they may or may not have.

If we consider the first person, who reacts in an active mode, we might develop different ideas about what she is doing on a sliding scale from acting with no inner space at all to acting out of much inner space. Her way of reacting could be the result of being so scared that she deliberately busies herself with activities. She knows that the more active she is, the less time she has for worrying and vexing herself with bad scenarios. She prefers to flee forward, organizing her own death and funeral instead of enduring the insecurity of not knowing what will happen. In this way she has the idea of controlling death.

Her activities might also be her normal way of responding to new situations. She has always been a very organized person who likes her personal things to be in order. So she starts organizing what has to be done just because it has to be done. Not so much out of an existential confrontation with her mortality, but rather from an attitude of doing one's duty. She is not so much a reflective person but more a practical person. What her dying means is not the most important question for her. She is more concerned with what it means for the people around her.

A third option might be that this person acts out of a great sense of inner peace. Yes, she will die in the near future, and therefore she is prepared to make this last phase of her life as much of a final personal goodbye as possible. She does not busy herself with activities in order not to think or feel, but she turns to activities in order to express her preferences and live life as fully as possible until its last moment.

As we see in these three possible interpretations of the active mode, there is much possible diversity on the active pole of the doing and undergoing spectrum. The *ars moriendi* model is not designed to measure which of these three versions is better or worse. It is there to create sensitivity to diversity and acknowledge and respect that people react in different ways.

Let us now turn to the other end of the spectrum and consider the person who kept living on as always. This might be the result of total shock and complete denial. The person cannot believe that her life is finite and she pretends to go on as always. Maybe the disease will just go away. Perhaps it was just a false diagnosis and things will turn out to be okay in the end. She does not feel anything, so why then believe what is being said? Physicians make mistakes too.

The same behaviour may also be the result of being a very practical and phlegmatic person. Things are as they are, and as long as there are no real symptoms one might as well go on living as one always has. Why worry about something one cannot influence? It does not bring anything good if you are too much in your head. Just keeping on doing keeps one off the street and is the best guarantee of doing well.

Another option might be that the person is very well connected to herself and enjoys every moment of her life. She is determined not to be affected by the fact that she will die in the near future. As the Greek philosopher Epicurus said: 'We should not be afraid to be death, for as long as I am alive death is not there, and when death is there I will no longer be alive.' Changing my behaviour would mean to succumb to death casting his shadow upon me. I want to live as consciously and fully to the last moment of my life. And death will not have anything of it, not an inch.

As we see, also the pole of undergoing may be lived and experienced differently according to the different ways in which inner space plays a role in a person's life. And there are even more options, for people might also be completely passive in the sense of lethargic and let everything fall out of their hands. They just sit there, feeling completely empty and do not know how to go on with their life. Undergoing then has the character of complete passivity, which can hardly be considered to be an intentional human action.

Having explored both poles of doing and undergoing and the many different faces they may have depending on how they are accompanied by inner space, we will now look for examples where both poles are integrated. The logic behind this is that the less inner space there is, the more the two poles will appear as extreme positions on a sliding scale. The more inner space there is, the more the two poles may be integrated.

A first example of a practice where doing and undergoing are (or should be) integrated is making music. When I play the piano I am actively engaged in moving my fingers in order to push the right keys on the keyboard. I become aware of how active I am and how much energy this costs on days when I feel ill. But simultaneously as I push the right keys, I am listening to the music I produce. I adapt my playing to what I hear and correct my speed and sound if necessary. If I play well, the music starts to take over, I begin to feel one with the instrument and it may even be that I feel so much part of the music that it seems as if the music plays itself through me. Doing and undergoing have been perfectly integrated into what is often called a flow.

A second example, which is related to suffering, comes from medieval theology. In the theology of Thomas Aquinas fortitude or courage is a virtue that is based on the more active capacity of our emotional life connected with power, energy and aggression. Through fortitude we have the right attitude in the face of danger: being able to face a dangerous or threatening situation without underestimating it (recklessness) or overestimating it (cowardice). Fortitude is the virtue par excellence connected with the greatest evil that can happen to people: death. Hence the virtue is associated with people not afraid to act in situations where their life is in danger, like firemen and soldiers. However, in his discussion as to what the most excellent act is to which fortitude can lead, Aquinas concludes that this should be martyrdom.

According to him it takes more courage to undergo a life-threatening danger for a good cause, knowing that one will not survive it, than resist the danger of death by powerful action. Hence, in martyrdom, doing and undergoing are completely integrated.

Having opened up the spectrum of doing and undergoing, let us return to Mr McNeal and see how he did having arrived at the palliative care unit.

Inner space

Five days after Mr McNeal entered the palliative care unit it was reported at the morning meeting that he was completely out of breath. He had been calling many times before a nurse finally appeared. He was given some morphine by mouth in order to take away the sensation of being out of breath. Injections caused him too much stress.

It was striking that he always sat in a chair in his room. He said that throughout his life he never slept much – no more than four hours a night. He did not want to lie down on the bed, as he said it would block his lungs. But after talking with him, staff established that he was afraid that once he lay down he would never get out of bed again.

He kept repeating, 'I eat well, I drink well.' Eating was a symbol for being alive. He tried to be in control all the time, knowing exactly what medication he had and what not. Because he still suffered from phlegm in his lungs – which he did not have the power to cough up – the doctor wanted to give him some antibiotics. According to Mr McNeal, however, antibiotics did not agree with him and made him sick. A morphine injection, to take away the tightness of the chest was not an option either: 'Then I will lie down and sleep forever.' They gave him morphine per mouth six times a day, with something to help reduce the slime in his lungs.

The old sailor resisted the idea that he was going to die soon and was probably more ill than he was prepared to show. At the same time he was very grateful for the care and safety offered to him. Despite the hopelessness of his situation he took great delight in small things. One of the things that he craved from time to time was a roll-up cigarette. He was allowed to smoke if someone was there with him. It was a curious ritual: the oxygen tube was hung away, the tap was closed, and he inhaled the smoke with the little air he still had in his lungs. He spoke with difficulty. His voice was almost gone. When we understood each other his eyes started to shine and he put his thumb up.

Regarding the positions between doing and undergoing, Mr McNeal was hard to pin down to one position. He seemed to be in control of his life and fought against the inevitable deterioration of his situation. Being used to taking the lead in life he had prepared himself by filling in a euthanasia declaration. From the moment he arrived at the palliative care unit, however, he never spoke about it. He underwent the slow progression of his disease, accepting his decreasing mobility, but refused to lie down and wait for the end. The two poles of doing and undergoing were both part of his behaviour. As long as he felt well in the unit and was allowed to smoke one of his roll-up cigarettes from time to time, he had no need to hasten death.

The dying process of Mr McNeal was no success story. It was not easy to gain access to him. He did not talk much and trying to set up a conversation about inner space was not something that made him feel comfortable. But with staff being very attentive to his pain and his fear of suffocating he was still able to experience life as worth living. By accepting himself the way he was, he could experience a space that did him good. As well as a cigarette he enjoyed a cup of coffee and the company of the nurses. From time to time his eyes started to shine: 'Nurse, it is so great to be here!' he'd say, and his big thumb would go up. Caring is being attentive and attuned, and in this case, accepting the limitations that were there. Inner space is as important for caregivers as it is for patients.

Total pain and total care

Palliative care approaches suffering as something that concerns the entire person, as is reflected in the concept of total pain. In all these dimensions, the poles of doing and undergoing play an important role. Considering the physical side of the dying process, one deals with a natural process of decline that has its own specific dynamism and development. Medicine can respond to this process in the way a gardener responds to the natural processes in a garden. Seeing a physician as a mechanic rather than a gardener leads to trouble in a number of ways.

In the first place, we might start to believe in the illusion that as long as we continue and replace everything we will not die. One of the problems of contemporary medicine is the fact that it is split up into so many sub-disciplines that tend to focus on one organ only, forgetting the complete picture. Someone may be treated for his breathlessness and praised for his strong heart, when at the same time his liver is under stress because of his excessive drinking caused by relational and social problems. Looking at the whole picture helps us remember that human beings are a unity and they are mortal as a unity. If parts are continually repaired without looking at the whole picture, people might manoeuvre themselves into a situation they never wanted. It takes courage to refuse to be treated for prostate cancer, because one does not want to die as a result of the dementia that has recently been diagnosed.

In the second place, we overestimate the power of physicians, making them responsible for what they are not responsible for and cutting off the possibility of undergoing as an alternative to being trapped in a logic of action. When a physician agrees with the patient and relatives that further chemotherapy would only prolong suffering and all agree to abstain from all live-saving measures, it is not the physician killing the patient, but the disease killing the patient. The decision might have been taken deliberately, and responsibility should be taken for allowing the disease killing the patient, but this can be justified by looking at the complete picture.

A third danger in comparing the physician with a mechanic rather than a gardener is related to the quality of caring. As care ethics teaches us, caring is a practice with more than one dimension (Heijst 2011). One of these dimensions can be called production: many actions that are part of the caring process have a technical side that can be measured and judged according to the outcome and separate from the process itself. Inserting a tube and making a stoma are examples of such actions. So far the comparison with technicians is possible. But caring has also the aspect of human actions that are judged by the quality of the intersubjective process itself, regardless of the outcome, like having dinner with friends or making love. There is (or should be) a difference between washing a car and washing a patient. And another dimension to caring as a practice is that it can express value in the way it is done. Washing a patient with love and respect may express how much this vulnerable fellow human being is valuable, despite the bad condition he or she is in.

What goes for the physical dimension of suffering also goes for the psychosocial and spiritual sides of the phenomenon. These are also processes with their own dynamism and speed. According to the technological rationality that is dominant in our culture, it is hard to see why suffering should be tolerated at all. If we have the power and possibility to treat suffering around the dying process in all its dimensions, do we not have a duty to do it? And if suffering cannot be treated by psychosocial or spiritual care, why then not accept the physical solution which consists of either bringing the patient to a state of unconsciousness by palliative sedation, or actively ending the life of the patient? Is our *ars moriendi* able to offer an alternative to this logic of action and is there something to say for that most extreme version of the undergoing pole, that is, suffering?

The problem of suffering

Writing about suffering is a precarious affair. It is easily forgotten that suffering as a generic category is an abstraction that tends to obscure the fact that in the real world human beings all suffer in their own individual way (Cassell 2004). Writing about suffering often ends up in the mind, forgetting the body as the most important access to the phenomenon.

As we have described in earlier chapters, we are our body and we have a body. The fact that these two are true at the same time remains a major mystery to our thinking. Our body is our boundary and point of contact with the surrounding world. When we are fit and healthy our body can enlarge our world, and when we do sports, perform music or make love, we may sometimes feel so connected with the world around us that we experience no more boundaries between ourselves and the rest of the world. When we suffer, however, the body may show its other face in a ruthless way. Experiencing severe pain, we feel our world shrinking. The body may be experienced as a part of us that feels no longer connected to who we are, an object, a burden, an entity that we want to get rid of. Simultaneously, however, it is precisely this alienating experience of ourselves that breaks down our world and who we are. It is precisely this that is intended in torture practices (Scarry 1985).

Although what we undergo is always mediated by the body, our bodily sensations are always experienced in interrelation with the psychosocial and spiritual dimension of our existence. Pain is experienced differently when others acknowledge that we have pain, and when they show empathy. People can suffer a lot when they have set their mind on finishing a marathon whatever it may cost. And some people intentionally seek the right amount of pain in order to experience sexual pleasure.

However, pain is hard to communicate, precisely because of its bodily situatedness. My unique body with its unique memory of everything I have experienced gives me a unique perspective on the world. This perspective cannot be transferred. A man can support his wife during childbirth in every possible way – bodily, psychosocially and spiritually – but he can never feel the pain she feels. However great their intimacy and however close they might be during the delivery, their bodies reveal themselves both as mediums of contact and boundary.

By radically taking the lived body as a point of departure when writing about suffering, we might avoid two ways of writing about suffering that block the effort to connect suffering with inner space. In the first way of writing, suffering is romanticized or idealized.

Suffering is seen as something that offers chances to grow, to be tested, to show one's character. In religious literature suffering may be presented that way – as an attractive vehicle for spiritual growth. The problem with this is that an ideal is constructed and expectations are formulated separate from reality. The attention is shifted from the insider perspective of the person who suffers towards an outsider perspective of a theory in which bad fate is sold as good luck.

The other way of writing that we want to avoid is the focus on suffering as fundamentally without any sense or meaning. This stance may be a reaction to the first way of writing about suffering and it may be an expression of solidarity with people who suffer from the first position. It forgets, however, that there are people whose suffering, through the years, has so much become a part of their identity that this view denies a part of their self. Again, people who really suffer are not helped, and an intellectual construction is built that is separated from real life, and prevents us from seeing what life may bring.

Both approaches to suffering may come from good intentions but they have a problematic relation to the meaningfulness of suffering, the first approach by emphasising too much meaning beforehand, and the second approach by blocking any possible meaning beforehand. Meaning, however, cannot be forced and is better served by inner space. Therefore, we propose that the best access to meaningfulness in suffering is the insider perspective. We will now hear from two witnesses.

The first witness is a Dutch female writer, Hannemieke Stamperius, who suffers severely from a bone disease. In an interview in a newspaper she says (Stamperius 2009):

> When I was diagnosed this bone disease twelve years ago, I was so frightened that I couldn't write for at least

half a year. I was also angry about what happened to me. Later I learned that this anger is 75% of the pain. The most important pain technique is: acceptance. Making that switch in your head: from not wanting to putting your will aside. Just being in the now, admitting the experience, waging no war against it, not surrendering either. Acceptance is an ongoing process, a searching for: how can I experience joy from this. ...I like to compare my relation with pain with a well-arranged wedding. You did not have a say in it at the beginning, but you make the best out of it. You have to take care of pain, approach it with love, make a good marriage out of it. Sometimes I can even laugh about all these physical sensations, from my neck to my feet, that are completely broke. Then I think: what a combination of chiming experiences. It may sound strange, but pain gives a deepening to life. ...Pain, silence and reflection are close to another. Pain is a kind of meditation. An emptying oneself and then an opening up. My inner life was not small, being the introvert I simply am, but now it is really of a different order. ...One of the consequences of pain is that you have a thinner skin, everything impresses much more. Reading is richer, music more subtle. The senses are being sharpened, emotions are more intense, one's entire existence gets filled with meaning. Because of pain nothing is noncommittal. Pain can be a mystical experience. (Translation: Carlo Leget)

The second witness is the photographer Hapé Smeele, who followed eight older people suffering from dementia in their last stage of life. In the preface to his book, he writes that the book is an answer to the question of the meaning of life, and especially the question of why there is so much pain in the world. This question urged itself on him as his son was prematurely born and appeared to suffer from an incurable disease. Smeele addresses himself to his son, who has already died (Smeele 2002):

> I would like to tell you how out of pain and sadness also beautiful things have grown, but I cannot do this by skipping the difficult, painful and sometimes bitter things. Because now I know that it is of great importance not to flee from the pain. Not by rubbing away the pain by saying e.g., 'Life goes on'. I know how tempting it is, if things go wrong, to go for it in order to change it all, taking control, or safeguard yourself by all means from future sadness. And thus to flee. Precisely by experiencing pain fully one can renew. Because that is what it comes down to. You do not just enter a new time, but you become a new human being. There is an appeal to talents of which you did not know you had. There is purification in that. But sometimes it is hardly bearable. …Your mother and I e.g., felt very clearly that we could react to your death by either becoming bitter, or seeking gentleness, love, emotion. There is no moment of decision in that. It is a knowing that grows and the feeling can change again and again. How did we come to such an answer? I still do not know. But it is not about a rational choice. I think we made it during and after your life through our love for each other, and by continuing to look for the gentleness. For myself, silence was added to that. Without silence I become all tied up and I lose the feeling of being supported and begin to think that I have to solve everything on my own. Then the depression and hardness come that create a distance to what can touch or move me at other times. If I then look for silence, the lightness comes of its accord. And I feel supported by the whole,

by creation. That is something new for me, I did not know that before. (Translation: Carlo Leget)

These two witnesses, however much the nature of their suffering may differ, have one thing in common: from their insider perspective they report how suffering is not a matter of undergoing in a passive way, but a complex interplay of being active, receptive, accepting and not surrendering. In this process, inner space plays a double role: it is needed for dealing with pain in a fruitful and constructive way, but it is also the fruit of this way of dealing with suffering.

In this chapter we have paid extra attention to the pole of undergoing, because the pole of doing is all too familiar to us, and we wanted to open a new space in our contemporary *ars moriendi*. Now we have seen how this might work in the case of suffering, might the same be applicable to the process of dying? Is there something like a natural death, characterized by undergoing, being the opposite of the unnatural death that exists in the active and intentional termination of life?

A natural death?

In one of her books Marie de Hennezel wrote of her 84-year-old mother-in-law who lived on her own at a camping site in the South of France (Hennezel 2000). Once a week she walked to the village to buy some cheese, vegetables and fruit. She was doing well for her age, having eaten all her life from her organic kitchen garden. When she sensed that the end was near, she stopped eating. She did take fluids in order not to dry out, but slowly she weakened and became less mobile. During her last weeks she was monitored by a physician so that any possible complication could be taken care of, and she was supported in her daily activities. After a month or two she died, peacefully, with a smile on her face.

Dying like this seems to be the perfect way of undergoing a natural death. No medical interventions, no pain and suffering, but a peaceful and slow transition from life to death. This image of dying has a great appeal to people living in industrialized highly technological countries. It harmonizes very well with an ecological spirituality that aims at more awareness of how we as human beings are part of nature. But does something like a natural death really exist at all?

Simone de Beauvoir, in a book about the dying of her mother, does not believe so (Beauvoir 1964). According to her, after the confrontation of death nothing is natural or self-evident anymore. Because of death we begin to ask questions about the world and we lose the naivety of our childhood. Everything we claim to be natural is in fact a cultural choice in which we use our skills and insights in order to use and manipulate nature so that we can enjoy it as much as possible without suffering from possible harms. We must not forget that the 84-year-old woman was monitored by a physician. Her natural death was a good death because it was embedded in medical care.

The British sociologist Jane Seymour has done research into the question of whether a natural death could still play a role in the highly technological environment of an intensive care unit in a hospital (Seymour 2000). Her findings are surprising. Even in an intensive care setting relatives consider the death of their beloved patients as natural provided that medical technology causes outcomes that they had expected: when this technology does not lead a life of its own but is used by the health carers; when the technological interventions can be understood by the general public; and when the way of dying fits in the overall picture of someone's life.

It seems, therefore, that the opposition between a natural death and a death mediated by medical technology is not a fruitful one to maintain. Finding a good balance between doing and undergoing seems to be a challenge at both ends of the spectrum. No patient is helped by overtreatment or undertreatment. But in order to find the right balance here, it might be helpful to reconsider with inner space one's actions on the spectrum of actions ranging from doing to undergoing, from active to passive.

Having come to the end of this chapter, how did Mr McNeal do in his last days? Almost two weeks after Mr McNeal had been admitted to the palliative care unit he woke up early at four o'clock in the morning. He had been sleeping in his bed for a week, and gradually his condition had worsened. Because he was short of breath and in a panic, a doctor was called. It was agreed that he would be kept asleep until the end. 'That injection won't kill me, will it?' he had asked. The physician had taken his hand and told him that it would only take him into a deep sleep. He had sunk back in his pillow and smiled at her. From that moment on he had been sleeping. He died later that day, in the company of his niece.

How Do I Say Goodbye?

When Betty was admitted to the palliative care unit she was in her mid-forties. With her short, straw-blond hair, a skinny appearance and eyes full of fear, it was clear that she was severely ill. Life had not treated Betty too well. Of the two children to whom she had given birth, one had died shortly after she was born and the other one had a mental disability due to lack of oxygen during childbirth. The girl was 15 years old now and difficult to handle. Although Betty was still legally married to the father, they were no longer living together. The divorce had been put on a hold from the moment that her incurable disease had presented itself.

Betty suffered a lot of pain. Most of the time she would sit in a chair, crooked and tensed, drinking coffee and staring out of the window. During the first two weeks there had been a lot of discussion in the team as to how she could be supported in such a way that she would relax and open up. After the nurses had given their best, the chaplain, the social worker and the psychologist had talked to her, she had been offered massage and aroma therapy and the music therapist had visited her, but she would not relax or give them a clue about why she was so tense. When she was given a shower by one of the nurses, an attractive young man in his early twenties, she suddenly opened up.

It appeared that she was worrying about her daughter. The girl was temporarily living with her grandfather, because her own father could not take care of her. It was unclear where the girl could stay when Betty was no longer there. Her grandfather and her husband did not get on well together. And now the girl had twice stolen money; she had bought guinea pigs, perfume and lipstick.

As I talked with Betty, she told me that she had become afraid of the dark. She had never had any problem with sleeping in the dark, but since her neighbour – a women in her late sixties – had died, she wanted a light on during the night. She had known the woman from the hospital, and they had been a great support for each other. Now she was gone, Betty was confronted with her own future. She felt deeply miserable with her situation. Everything seemed broken: her body, her marriage, her daughter, her future. She did not know what to do. She was determined not to die. But she felt that her disease took more and more of the power she needed to put things in order.

Death takes away everything we have and everything we are. How do we deal with this? What is the best way of responding to the feeling that everything is lost? One is inclined to think that dying is a process in which we all have to learn to let go of life. Letting go seems to be the primary task for both the dying patients and their relatives. Both seem to be in a process of grief. But does this represent the whole picture of the dying process, or is it a one-sided view?

When one of my colleagues met a woman whose husband had died six months ago she expressed her sorrow and told her she admired the way she was dealing with it. She knew it had been a good marriage, and could imagine how hard it was to let go of a beloved husband. The woman's reaction was unexpectedly critical of her well-meant words.

She said that she was thoroughly fed up with all those people who praised her because she was apparently so successful in letting go of her husband. He still meant a lot to her and she was not determined to let go of him. Precisely because he still meant so much to her, she was able to go on with life, happy to still be connected with her great love.

In this chapter we will challenge the widespread idea that the process of dying is basically a process of letting go. In our new *ars moriendi* we will place the way we deal with the good things in life between two poles: holding on and letting go. We will show that these two poles can help us to see how the grief experienced by both the patient and the family can be multi-dimensional and polyphonic. Depending on the inner space present, the characteristics of holding on and letting go may differ, as we have seen in preceding chapters with regard to other tensions. But let us first take a look at how contemporary culture deals with the poles of holding on and letting go with regard to the good things in life.

A society of well-preserved consumers

With the effective use of penicillin and more hygienic lifestyles after World War II people started to live to be older in the North Atlantic world. In Germany at the end of the nineteenth century retirement age was fixed at the age of 65, which was the average life expectancy of Germans at the time. Today, people dying at that age are considered to die too young. We live longer, look younger and stay in better health than any generation that lived before us. In fact, a whole science and industry has been developed in order to support successful ageing, and with the psychological taboo on dying being prevalent, there seems no need to think about letting go of life.

Extending the human life span and preserving youthfulness foster a mentality of holding on rather than letting go. And this is supported by many medical and technological developments that help us to continue drinking from the eternal fountain of youth – cosmetic surgery and the use of Viagra to name but a few. As a result of this culture of preservation, there is a large majority of people who are not prepared to think about living wills or the prospect of dying. There are also many many people who have told nobody what their wishes would be if they were to have an accident and arrive at hospital unconscious.

However, there also seem to be a growing number of older citizens who are still healthy but who nevertheless do not consider their life worth living anymore. Although physically their process of ageing has been successful, they live in 'a tangle of inability and unwillingness to connect to one's actual life' (Wijngaarden *et al.* 2016, p.265). This psychosocial and spiritual suffering makes them think about ending their lives or even actually planning a self-inflicted death. The same development is seen with regard to people who fear the suffering of dementia. The fear of suffering from this disease in the near future causes many people to reflect on how they can leave their situation before they are no longer the person they were during the majority of their lifetime.

These existential struggles can be described within the framework of the preceding tensions: the more one's relation with oneself is becoming fragile or even disappears, the more one's personal identity is held up by the interpersonal and institutional dimensions – a horrifying scenario for many people. Or in terms of doing and undergoing, people find it hard to undergo such a process of losing their meaning in life and their identity.

Many people in that situation start to think about doing something about it: in countries where physician-assisted dying is legal, they fill in euthanasia declarations pro-actively, just in case it is the only way out. In terms of the tension central to this chapter, one could say that these people are ready to hold on to life as long as life treats them well. But if life becomes too hard, they are ready to let go in a very radical way.

This brings us to a closer reflection about letting go. Is this really what is happening in cases like this? Isn't this attitude of 'not like this' rather a form of 'throwing away' that is far more widespread in our culture than letting go? We live in a consumer society that continuously trains us to be unsatisfied with our situation. Advertising makes us believe that we either miss something important that will make us happier or have better options or possibilities available to us. In both cases we are told to stop using a particular product or provider and exchange it for something else. Neoliberalism has taught us to be unsatisfied customers who should be continuously searching for better and cheaper options, being prepared to throw away what we already have. And throwing away and replacing things has become a major imperative for those who would like to stay up to date. Technology is developing so rapidly that the mobile phones we use are designed to be replaced every two years. The same goes for many other devices that we have become accustomed to.

The Polish–British sociologist Zygmunt Bauman has framed our age as 'liquid modernity', meaning that we live with no permanent bonds, being flexible in our roles in society and flowing through our own life like tourists (Bauman 2000). We are no longer attached and committed to lifelong relationships and loyalties, but continuously adapt to new developments, new situations and new chances. Our normative mindset is on shifting rather than staying. And shifting involves letting go in a specific way.

In order to develop a more precise framework for understanding the tension between the poles of holding on and letting go we will focus some more on these terms and see how they can change depending on how they are connected with inner space.

Holding on and letting go

As we have seen before, in the case of the tension between doing and undergoing, both poles can be opposites representing incompatible positions, and there are ways in which both poles can be integrated. In the case of holding on and letting go, one can see the same phenomenon. There are ways of holding on that are completely opposite to letting go. Someone hanging on a cliff and trying to preserve his life clings to the cliff and should hold on to it. Letting go of the rock would mean he would lose his life.

This image of holding on illustrates very well why there is no inner space involved: there is only one option here, there are no alternatives, and any openness would directly endanger the situation. This way of holding on resembles that of the humourless dictator or fundamentalist, denying any other view on reality that differs from their view. Holding on has the character of clinging to, stubborn and determined. The image is one of holding an object so tightly that it is squeezed.

The opposite of this kind of holding on without inner space, is any form of letting go without inner space. Here the act is likewise stubborn and determined, without any other option. Letting go in this sense has the character of throwing away. Holding on is not an option and one should get rid of it. The image here is that of a hand throwing a baseball: opening up, but with the aim of letting go as quickly as possible.

But there are other ways of letting go that are of a different character. Take, for example, the letting go of a child who learns to walk or ride a bike. Holding on is no longer necessary, even hindering the process, and the hand is opened so that a kind of freedom is generated. Or take the example of a small bird that is caught between two hands. When the hands are opened, the bird is free to go, nothing holding it, but also nothing pushing or throwing it away. Inner space is there as absolute openness. Whether the bird flies away or stays, it is okay.

This openness of letting go can also have a direction, in the case of someone giving or offering something. Buying someone a present and giving it to them is an example of letting go with an intention. Inner space is filled here with feelings of friendship, gratitude or love. It is still an open gesture, for nothing is asked in return, but there is a certain direction as well. The gift is given trusting that it will do some good to someone. There is always the risk that the gift is not accepted, which makes the giver vulnerable. But if the gift is given with openness, it will not disappoint the giver.

The same open and trusting attitude can be found in someone surrendering. We all know this from falling asleep or relaxing deeply. And here as well we can imagine that there are ways of surrendering in which one gives oneself away trusting that one is being received well. Think of the surrendering out of love which happens when people make love, or when someone dies believing that they will be received by the loving hands of God.

Just as we have seen the character of letting go change when there is more inner space, the same can be said with regard to holding on. For next to clinging on or squeezing, there are ways of holding on that are in a perfect balance between too tight and too loose. Swinging an axe when chopping wood is only successful when the right balance is found: holding too tight one will lose the swing that generates the power needed to split the wood; holding too loose one runs the risk of losing the axe. Needed here is the right middle ground that we also know from studying the virtues.

Other forms of holding on are open to letting go. The same hand of a father teaching his son to walk or ride a bike is there as a hold, a support that is ready to let go if necessary. And the image of the bird which is held, offering it the freedom to fly as it likes, has the same character of inner space.

Also, these forms of holding on can have a direction and an intention. The holding on which is found in honouring someone is similar to the present that we talked about. In fact what we see here is that in this example there is both holding on and letting go simultaneously. There seems to be a perfect integration of the two.

How this can be practised at the end of life is well illustrated by a story that one of my former colleagues once told me. When his first wife died of cancer, during the last hours of her life he had caressed her with his hand on her lower arm in order to express both his love for her and his support during her suffering. Suddenly, however, he realized that caressing her arm with the inside of his hand might express too much desire to keep her with him. Her death was inevitable, so he wanted to express both his nearness and support on the one hand, and her freedom to let go of life on the other. The solution he found was caressing her arm with the outside of his hand, expressing holding on and letting go in one gesture.

Although both poles of the tension can be integrated at times, the combination of holding on and letting go can also be expressed in a more polyphonic way: allowing some inner voices to extinguish while we give other voices more space to develop. Or, as the American bioethicist Daniel Callahan expressed it in an image with regard to ageing: the art of ageing well is like the art of preserving a bouquet of flowers (Callahan 1988). After one week you take out the flowers that have faded, in order to give the remaining flowers more space to flourish. Here holding on and letting go appear as opposite actions, but simultaneously performed and equally important for the result that is intended.

What can this reflection tell us with regard to Betty's situation? What options come into view concerning her lack of inner space and the way she suffered in her situation?

Inner space

Betty was in an almost impossible situation to let go of life. Dying is letting go of everything one has and is. Confronted with the question: 'Who are you and what do you really want?' Betty would formulate her answer completely in terms of the other-pole. First and foremost she was the mother of her 15-year-old daughter who had stolen money to comfort herself and recompense her for the difficult situation she found herself in, being (as she felt it) abandoned by her mother and her father. Betty defined and experienced herself primarily through the relationship with her daughter, and from that perspective it was clear to her that there was only one option: to cling on to life as long as possible, to make sure that her daughter would be okay after her death. The me-pole, connected with her unfinished life story, was to a far lesser degree important to her. True, she had to write the final chapter of her life story in her mid-forties, something she had hoped to do some forty years later. But the pain of this fact was not related to the idea that she had so many plans for her life – she had never felt that there was much to choose in life – as she had plans for her daughter. So for Betty, taking away the insecurity about where her daughter would live, and how the girl would be supported in school, would have a direct impact on her pain and anxiety.

Since people are connected in a life-sustaining web, Betty's close relatives – her daughter, her husband, her parents – were not in a position to let her go either. Her daughter needed her mother more than anything. Whether her theft was a way of screaming for attention, a self-destructive act, a way of getting money to comfort herself, or a combination of all three did not matter so much. It was clear that the girl was as much in despair as her mother.

Betty's parents did what they could in order to take care of their daughter and granddaughter. And her husband was in a complex process of feeling guilty towards the woman he had planned to divorce but who had suddenly fallen incurably ill. Of all the relatives he was the most unpredictable one, switching from anger and quarrelling with his father-in-law, to feeling sorry for Betty and trying to organize something that she could look forward to.

And finally, also the caregivers felt as if they were confronted with a hopeless situation. Many of them were the same age as Betty and identified with her in many respects. For them, as well, the situation was hard to cope with and asked much of their inner space.

If we look at Betty through the lens of the three polarities of the new *ars moriendi* we have discussed, one could say that she was at the other-pole rather than at the me-pole with regard to who she was and what she really wanted; more at the undergo-pole than the do-pole with regard to how she dealt with suffering; and more at the holding on-pole than the letting go-pole with regard to saying goodbye. With regard to all of these poles there seemed to be little inner freedom or inner space. And this was reflected in the way her body was tense and stressed.

Looking at Betty's inner life from this perspective, one could begin to investigate how she could be facilitated to develop some more inner space. It was clear that first of all her greatest worries needed to be met. How could a safe place for her daughter be found, a place where she knew her daughter would be loved and taken care of? In order to answer this question we need to look at the life-sustaining web of relations around Betty and her daughter. The father and the grandparents were needed as important players who could inform what possibilities there were.

But the second question was equally important. How could Betty be helped to be an agent, someone in control and not just passively undergoing, in those areas she wanted to be an agent? If Betty had always led a life in which other people were the ones initiating and she responding, there was no use in trying to change her in her last weeks. But there might be specific subjects or issues in which she would like to have a more active role, but didn't know where to start.

And this brought us to the first question: Who am I and what do I really want? Betty was inclined to define her identity first and foremost as being a mother. But of course she was more than her role. She was a mother in her own specific and unique Betty-way. Bringing her closer to this would help her connect more with the me-pole of her identity. By being more consciously connected with herself and her life story, she could be invited to think about what she wanted to tell her daughter for later life, or how she wanted to be remembered. There were many ways in which she could do this, such as writing letters to her daughter for specific occasions like her eighteenth and twenty-first birthdays or her wedding day. But whatever forms there were to work with these tensions, the most important thing in our new *ars moriendi* was that Betty's inner space was the point of departure. The major task of the caregivers was to learn to live with seeing possibilities and solutions that the dying person does not want.

Almost three months after being admitted to the palliative care unit, Betty died. Her daughter had visited her many times, and Betty was relatively reassured that she was taken care of well. Her husband had tried to organize a boat trip for her that did not succeed because of the weather. Until the very end she suffered from severe pain. But she chose to die that way in order to be clear and close to the people she loved. As the chaplain formulated it: 'She confronted us with the question: Can you accept that I cannot accept it?' He also told us that her parents had been at her bedside during one of those last nights. Their sweet tenderness had struck him. 'It was as if they had been watching over her, guarding near her cradle. In those times, more than forty years ago, surprised, now baffled, but no less caring.' Their sorrow was beyond words. There are no words for the pain you feel when your own child dies. Betty had experienced this herself before.

On dying and bereavement

Although the patient is the central player in the new *ars moriendi*, again and again we have seen how important the relatives are. In that sense the art of dying is more like learning to play the first violin in a quartet than learning to play solo. The violins and the cello play their part and every instrument co-determines how the other instruments sound. With regard to saying goodbye at the end of life, both patients and relatives are caught in the tension between holding on and letting go. This process starts during the period of illness and continues for the relatives in the bereavement phase after the moment of death.

Grief is not something that is only experienced after someone has died. Grief is a normal response to any loss that people may experience in their lives. People who die also experience grief, although there might not always be a mourning period during which they adapt to the loss. Because the new *ars moriendi* is a model that might help both patients and relatives, and because grief is part of the process of holding on and letting go, what can be said about this subject in relation to inner space?

Being confronted with grief and mourning, one will inevitably run into four ideas that are widespread and are repeated again and again and copied without question because they seem so self-evident (Bout 1999). Let us summarize them briefly:

- Mourning consists of a number of phases of grief you have to go through.

- During these phases all kinds of negative emotions will be experienced (anger, grief, guilt, and so on).

- You will have to work through these emotions with great awareness so that you can cut the bond with the deceased person.

- After about a year your life will gain balance again and you can finish your bereavement.

The problem with this widespread image of mourning is that although there may be people for whom this is an accurate description of their mourning process, it cannot be generalized and taken for granted that everyone will experience a similar process. Even worse, because this image is so dominant, it may keep the unique mourning process of specific individuals out of sight and neglect their personal way of mourning. Let us take a closer look at these four ideas and what their value might be:

- The idea that mourning consists of a number of stages of grief is based on the work of Elisabeth Kübler-Ross (1969). Although in her earlier work she presented the idea of five stages of grief that everyone would have to go through (denial, anger, bargaining, depression, acceptance), in her later work she nuanced this idea to the thought that these are aspects of grief that can be experienced in any order. The existence of stages of grief that one has to go through has never been confirmed by any long-term empirical research. It may be true that grieving implies a number of tasks (Worden 2002). Accepting the reality of the loss, for example, is a task that every grieving person has to perform, but enduring pain and sorrow is not necessarily something that everyone has to go through. Adapting to a new life without the lost one is clearly a task that everyone has to work on. Whatever tasks there may be, they cannot be ticked off like a shopping list. For this reason, other researchers prefer to speak about a dual process in which those who grieve go through a process of oscillation between stressors that relate directly to the death and the feelings associated with it on the one hand, and stressors that deal with restoration, like the acquisition of new roles and relating to friends and family in new ways, on the other hand (Stroebe and Schut 1999).

- The idea that in mourning all kinds of negative emotions will be experienced is also just a part of reality. Sometimes to their surprise and confusion, people feel relieved, or even happy. But how does one deal with such feelings that do not fit into the societal picture of someone who mourns? Many people will not understand this and even be shocked. Some survivors therefore complain that only in bereavement groups do they feel that they are allowed to laugh.

- But if there are negative emotions, do we have to work through them so that the bond of the deceased can be cut off? Again, the answer is not necessarily. There are people who do not have to deal with their negative emotions. They have a different way of mourning. And the bond with the deceased does not have to be cut off. Since the 1990s it has been accepted that continuing bonds with the deceased can be of great importance (Klass, Silverman and Nickman 1996). I remember one of the older women in the nursing home who had a small black-and-white picture of a two-year-old boy on the wall next to her bed. As I asked her about it she told me it was one of the rare pictures of her son who had drowned at the age of two, 56 years ago. As she told me this, her eyes slowly filled with tears and her mouth trembled.

- Finally, is there a fixed time – perhaps a year – after which life regains its balance? Again, we are dealing with a widespread misunderstanding. Of course it would be great if one could know when the wound of mourning would be healed, but it is dangerous to settle on any time periods here. The diversity between people is enormous and what one person lives through within months or even years, takes a couple of weeks for someone else. This can be painful or hard to understand for those who are around the grieving person, but emotional processes follow their own individual timeframe.

Recognition of the uniqueness of the griever is perhaps the most important of the new insights that have been accepted by researchers, although this can be hard to spread in society. What do these new insights into grief and mourning mean for our new *ars moriendi*? In a sense they only underline the importance of inner space in the case of grief and mourning. In grief, people experience the tension between holding on and letting go in many different ways. Inner space helps them to live with the confusing and unpredictable experience of dealing with loss and readapting to a new life. But inner space also helps us to have patience with those experiencing the personal and unique process of losing a loved one.

7

How Do I Look Back on My Life?

The first time I saw Michael from a close distance I was shocked: he was a man in his early thirties, emaciated, with a strange swollen belly. I had seen him from time to time, riding on his nursing home scooter up and down to the restaurant. But now I sat in front of him, in his room. As I looked at his face, I saw a skull. It was mainly his bones that gave shape to his head. Hollow-eyed, he talked slowly and monotonously. In the picture that was hanging on the wall behind him, he proudly held up an enormous pike-perch in one hand. He loved fishing and he used to go out with friends during the weekends. Stomach cancer had turned a healthy young man into a wreck in no more than a year and a half.

Initially, I found it hard to make contact with Michael, but as I got involved with his daily care I began to feel a kind of connectedness. I helped the nurses with showering and dressing him, and after a while I was able to help him on my own. He began to tell me about his life, about his two young children who visited him regularly, about the mother of his children (the women he had divorced), and about his new girlfriend who had dropped him like a hot potato when she learned of his incurable disease.

Gradually I familiarized myself with the small world of a terminal patient: the accuracy with which his bed had to be made, so that there would be no folds or creases; the enormous joy of a cup of coffee; the importance of the coffee being at the right temperature; the great importance of small things.

Michael had asked for euthanasia. Not because he wanted to die. 'Every day is still another day, isn't it?' he used to say. But it gave him peace of mind to know that he would not have to suffer any longer if he was going to lie there contorted with pain. The injections had already been prepared. The physician had told me that in his case at any moment there could be a crisis that would make his situation untenable.

Michael carried on living for weeks. He became more and more emaciated, had more difficulty speaking and had greater pains when swallowing. 'His will to live keeps him alive,' they used to say on the ward. In the last week I worked on the palliative care unit I told him I would be leaving in a couple of days. He started to talk about his fear of dying; about his children who understood precisely what was happening; his son whose anger would suddenly flare up, and his daughter who would suddenly start to cry or want to hug him. He told me that he had not seen his children for some time, since shortly after the divorce. His wife did not want them to meet his new girlfriend. Again he began to talk about death, his fear of the unknown. 'You know,' he said, 'when I am dead, I imagine sitting on top of my coffin and seeing everything.'

Michael died a week after I had finished my work at the palliative care unit. One of the carers told me that in the evening before his death his pain had increased. He had asked for an extra dose of morphine, which had been administered to him. It seems as if he had seen it coming for he had asked his ex-wife to stay. She had not been able to because of the children, and of course she felt guilty afterwards. That night, at three o'clock he was found dead. He had died alone.

A few days later Michael was buried. I attended the funeral with some colleagues from the ward. As we entered the chapel of the cemetery there was music playing: 'Only the good die young'. After everyone had been seated, the master of ceremonies announced that Michael had prepared an audiotape. Suddenly his slow and monotonous voice was there again. He started to welcome everyone and joked that he could see all of us sitting there. I had to think about his remark a week ago about sitting on top of his coffin. Then he started to say goodbye to all of us: his children ('Daddy is in heaven now...be sweet to mummy...I hope you will do better than me'); his ex-wife ('I still love you, despite everything...'); his friends ('Remember when we said we would fix our car, but ended up in the pub... Remember that party with those ladies... Sorry about what happened at your engagement party... Be sweet to your mother, and fix up that old house of hers...'); his father ('Dad, put your life back on track... take my example: if I can fight, you can make it as well...'). The theme of his speech was that it was important to keep fighting, but also that he hoped that others would do better than him and that they had deserved a better life.

Michael was an ordinary guy, one out of many. He was a young man who fell mortally ill in the middle of his life and felt screwed up by life. As he saw the many loose ends and ruptures that came to the surface, he tried to turn them in a positive direction in his own way. The audiotape at his funeral was his way of taking responsibility and having one last chance to put things right.

A society of shiny happy people

One of the fundamental cultural changes that marked the 1960s was the rise of an ideal of democratization that was accompanied by a rejection of authority. In music, arts and fashion a popular culture arose that was rebellious towards traditional conventions and transgressed these in every possible way by the consumption of drugs, free sex and loud music. Students occupied university buildings and demanded to have a say in the design of the study programmes and the decisions that until then had been made by university boards. And even in the churches a new spirit was sensed that reflected this culture of democratization. In the hierarchic and highly traditional Roman Catholic Church, for example, in many countries the traditional Holy Mass in Latin was replaced by liturgies in the local languages of the countries where people lived; lay people started to take part in the preparation of these liturgies, and in many churches drumkits with long-haired young people chased the traditional churchgoers away from their Sunday morning rituals.

The impact of these anti-authoritarian and democratic developments can hardly be overestimated and is still being continued, developed and merchandized in new forms. What is important for this chapter is the fact that they initiated a new approach to morality. Traditionally morality was seen as something that was upheld by institutions. The Churches, for example, commented on societal developments and contributed to the societal debate by playing the role of a moral compass. By declining any external authority, people looked for a new orientation and found it inside themselves. Either one's conscience or one's feelings became a new foundation for morality, and authenticity became a new moral ideal that was based on the flourishing of the unique individual rather than institutions.

The shift from the institutional to the individual in matters of morality was paralleled and endorsed by a shift from the religious to the psychological. Traditionally, religion in north western Europe had framed morality in terms of responsibilities and duties. Failing to meet these one would sense feelings of guilt. This was seen as a natural and healthy reaction to a transgression of a moral commandment. It proved that one possessed a well-developed conscience. With the fighting of taboos and the rise of psychology, however, guilt was seen as something unhealthy, promoting feelings of depression and unhappiness. Guilty feelings could be dealt with in therapy, and people could be liberated from an internalized morality that did not correspond with their individual authentic feelings. Where the old moral ideal was to be free of sins and guilt (remember the devils in the medieval *ars moriendi* holding up a list of sins that had been committed during life), the new moral ideal was to work on one's self-development or self-actualization.

Interestingly, this new moral ideal created new forms of pressure. Man had to be liberated from all kinds of external morality and taboos in order to become a free authentic individual. In the third chapter we met this development in the form of a shift from the other-pole to the me-pole. With regard to the subject of this chapter – how to deal with the things in life that have not gone well or were even morally false, bad or wrong – we will frame it in the tension between remembering and forgetting.

Where traditional morality focused on remembering the sins that had been committed in the past in order put things right, the new morality focused on forgetting what had been done in order to work towards a future of self-actualization. In Chapter 2 we discussed different ways of looking at morality: traditional morality is more like a road map from which past transgressions can be read, whereas the new morality is more similar to an acorn that develops into a unique tree. Both approaches coexist, offering different perspectives on guilt and happiness.

The paradox of self-actualization as a duty is that again an external moral pressure appears, the criterion of which is placed inside the unique individual (Taylor 1991). Only I can find out how I can develop into the authentic individual I am supposed to be. Because of the subjectivist nature of the enterprise, emotions and feelings become an important moral compass. When it 'feels good', when it is according to 'my truth', when it accords with 'my authentic self', then it should be good. There is no external moral authority to judge it, for every person has his or her own truth.

The duty of self-actualization is accompanied with another duty that paradoxically causes an external pressure: the duty to be happy. Happiness is something that we psychologically understand and even perform research on at universities. We know what it is and it is one's own responsibility to work on it in order to become a happy person. Being happy is feeling well. There are many ways to reach this goal, either by working hard or just being lucky. And if one feels depressed, there are therapies to make one feel good again. Everything can be fixed.

But what about cultural backgrounds other than a traditional Christian one? Does the same story apply to people who come from a culture of shame as opposed to a culture of guilt? It is true that there is a great difference between a culture of guilt, in which the judgement I have on myself plays a central role, and a culture of shame, in which the judgements other people have on me are decisive. In cultures where the community is more important than the individual – such as Morocco or Japan – the fear of losing face is the external compass that directs moral conduct. In essence, however, we deal here with the same logic of remembrance: what has been done wrong should be punished and made right. Although the new morality of self-actualization originated in the 1960s, the two ways of looking at right and wrong, remembering and forgetting, still exist and are part of our everyday life. One way of holding up morality as a society is by legal regulation, and no policeman will be convinced if one says one just had to ignore the red light or the speed limit because it was important to one's self-actualization. And the tabloid press makes much money exploiting the shame of celebrities, no matter what their individual idea of happiness is.

Dealing with guilt, right and wrong in the North Atlantic world has become a complex issue in which a number of subcultures with their own moral orientations clash. Someone who is getting divorced may be praised by one group of friends because she has the courage to choose for herself, whereas another group of her friends feels that she has not done enough to save her marriage, and a third says they have no judgement because they feel that this is just the way life goes. Often these diverse moral orientations are found in one person. In our inner life they are a polyphony in which different moral positions are presenting themselves. That brings us to the issue of inner space again.

Remembering and forgetting

In looking back on our life we are focusing on the past. Many people have this need when they feel their life is ending. It is connected with the need to understand who one was and what one really wants, which is partly met by finishing one's life story. We discussed this in Chapter 4. Focusing on the past may work out differently in different people. For some people, focusing on what has been is like visiting a treasure chamber, piled with great memories of their golden age. For others, thinking about the past runs the risk of exposing them to previous traumatic events. People might have different motives for wanting or refusing to look back on their life.

If we reflect on the many ways in which we can relate to past events, we could say that they can be organized in the spectrum between the two poles of remembering and forgetting. Again, we will discover a great variety of positions, depending on how much inner space exists.

If we start with the pole of remembering, one can imagine that in its most extreme form people are so much fixated on the past that it keeps them from confronting the here and now. The older bank director in Chapter 3 is a good example of someone who needed to focus on the societal position he once had in order to maintain his self-respect. This can be the case with regard to one's golden age, but it can also apply to something difficult that has happened.

One of the older men in the nursing home wrestled with his conscience so heavily that it occupied all his attention and prevented him from looking at his actual situation. Long ago he had betrayed his wife with another woman, and he had never had the nerve to tell her. His wife had died some months ago and now he reproached himself for never having spoken about it. The untold secret manifested itself as an obstruction to the continuing bond with his wife. The chaplain suggested that he could speak to his wife, addressing the photograph of her that was standing on his bedside table. This was a possibility he had never thought of. After an emotional 'conversation' he felt inner space that helped him to deal with what he blamed himself for.

With more inner space, the fixation on the past may develop towards a form of remembering that does not take away the pain or shame completely, but helps us to live with it. Compare it to the image of the bird sitting in an open hand, as we discussed in the previous chapter. Inner space may help us to see what happened in the past as something that is over now and does not need to be revisited if it does not help to make the actual or future situation better.

In the same way, at the other end of the spectrum, the practice of forgetting may have different faces depending on how it is connected with inner space. In its most extreme form, forgetting may have the character of suppressing or even erasing the thought of what has happened in the past. If memories are too painful, it may be impossible to live with them and there is no choice left but to cover them. There is no inner space at all, and no tolerance. This extreme way of forgetting may happen unknowingly, in the way the psyche may suppress a traumatic event, or it may be an intentional strategy in order to survive or to be able to live with oneself. It also may be a way of denying responsibility for one's past actions, reframing them as the stepping stones necessary to develop into the person one is now.

But forgetting may also have a different appearance when there is more inner space involved. Forgetting may also represent leaving what once was in the past, because it has no more meaning in actual life. It may be a mild and generous way of looking at a past situation, accepting it as it was, and leaving it there.

As we see, with the increase of inner space, the two poles of remembering and forgetting can become less opposed and more integrated with each other. This integration can be achieved in different ways. In the first place, there is a kind of integration that is achieved when one is able to live with the inner polyphony; the different voices inside oneself, blaming and understanding or excusing, coexist and reflect the many ways in which a situation can be understood. There is no need for a final judgement but rather acceptance of life in its many aspects.

The second way in which remembering and forgetting can be integrated is through reconciliation or forgiveness. Being able to forgive is a sign of inner space. One is no longer chained to the past, either by being fixated on it or supressing it. In the case of forgiveness there is both a moment of remembering – what went wrong in the past is brought to the present – and a moment of forgetting – after it has been acknowledged, it is put back in the past. Forgiveness closes past chapters in order to open new chapters. When Nelson Mandela was asked how he could forgive the guards that held him captive for all those years, he answered: 'As I walked out the door toward the gate that would lead to my freedom, I knew if I didn't leave my bitterness and hatred behind, I'd still be in prison.'

Forgiveness is something that can open up the future and as such it can be a great gift for those who are left behind. Because it is sometimes so hard to achieve, rituals can help in bringing it about. But rituals only work if they connect to a person's mental and emotional situation. One of the older men in the nursing home was dying and the family had asked for a ritual to say farewell to him. The old man had a difficult character and he kept on resisting the terminal situation he was in. Communication with him had been a challenge, for he had never wanted to talk about things. Respecting his state of mind, the chaplain had written a psalm of protest for him, a text in which his dissatisfaction with life was expressed and which could be shared with the family members. Having read the psalm, the chaplain asked the man if there was something else he wanted to say or share. Suddenly something completely unexpected happened – the man expressed his love towards his wife. It was an intimate moment. In an almost natural way the eldest son took over the lead in the ceremony. At that moment the youngest son started sobbing. He started talking: his father had never been there for him and he had always felt like the black sheep in the family. That utterance paved the way for reconciliation between the father and his youngest son.

Inner space

The central question of this chapter is: 'How do I look back on my life?' When Michael was confronted with this question, he did something extraordinary. He looked at the good things and the bad things in his life and decided to give them a positive turn. In his post-mortal farewell speech he addressed the most important people in his life personally, he expressed his feelings towards them by either telling them how much he cared about them, or how much he wished them to better their lives and do what he could no longer do.

Michael's speech was a text that had been prepared with much inner space. He was clear about what had been fun and what had gone wrong in his life, he apologized where he thought this was needed, and he did not try to kick anyone in the ass. And with this we discover something new about inner space. During the first days I had known Michael I did not have the impression that he was in the possession of much inner space. He was afraid to die and easily bothered when things were different from his expectations or hopes. At the same time, when he looked back on his own life, he turned out to possess a lot of inner space. This shows that, interestingly, with regard to inner space people may also be polyphonic, being quite relaxed and open in one area and very closed and stressed in another.

If we look at Michael's speech against the background of the polarity between remembering and forgetting, we see that here he seems to be neither chained to the past nor in need of suppressing memories. Although he could not accept that he would die at a relatively young age, he had the ability to look back on his life in a mature way. With this he helped the people he left behind enormously.

This brings us to the role of the relatives with regard to remembering and forgetting. Building on what we have said about the intrinsic relational nature of human identity in Chapter 4, we might suspect that the process of finding a balance in life is never merely an individual matter. One's own answer to the question: 'How do I look back on my life' may be completely different from the answer other people would give. In palliative care both patient and relatives are at the focus of attention and ideally both parties share a common view. To deal with the dimension of past and future and the role of time, let us take a look at the following story, taken from my diary.

Time

1 July – Today I met Mr Johnson, a man in his late sixties, reconciled with his fate and patiently waiting for his death. Two weeks ago there was a farewell ritual with his wife, children and grandchildren. According to the physician the way he is quietly living towards the end of his life is very special.

3 July – This morning we bathed Mr Johnson. He is a kind, quiet man. He has a cachectic syndrome and a dry and black sense of humour. He was bothered by two washing bowls that were on his sink. 'I think they are meant for tomorrow,' I said. 'That is rather premature,' he responded.

9 July – Mr Johnson is really waiting. He is not very approachable. Everything has been said, he has said farewell to his family and now it seems he has ended up in a black hole. He is easily irritated by small things. He does not want his grandchildren to visit him anymore. He has told the chaplain that he feels the end coming nearer.

15 July – At the end of the afternoon there was a meeting with Mr Johnson's family without the man himself. The chaplain started the meeting by inviting all who were present to tell how they were doing. His wife said she could not bear it any longer. The situation had been lasting for years now, first with care at home and now in the nursing home. They had said goodbye four weeks ago and now she had to say goodbye again every day as if it were the last day. She was completely worn out. The children said that their mother would not show how tired she really is. Sharing these experiences was a great relief. It appeared that all children visited their father, but did not talk about it among themselves. This meeting helped to share experiences and find some resilience. The conversation took more than one and a half hours, and many things about the past came up. Mr Johnson had been on a psychiatric ward. Strange things had happened there. He had had strange bruises and one day he had almost jumped out of a window. His family suspected the doctors of covering things up.

17 July – The atmosphere is tense. Mr Johnson is at the unit as a palliative care patient, but behaves more and more like a chronic patient. Everyone has difficulties shifting down to a chronic time experience, having said goodbye to a terminal patient.

1 August – During the team meeting a great discrepancy appeared between the friendly atmosphere during the farewell ritual in the chapel in the middle of June and Mr Johnson's difficult marriage. 'If I had known everything beforehand, I would not have married him,' his wife had said. The man is hard to follow at times – he complains about pain in his belly to his family, yet he assures the nurses that his pain has gone. Is he afraid to disappoint the nurses or does his family cause him stomach ache? From these conversations the portrait arises of a man who has always been the one in charge and is not willing to change this.

7 August – More and more it becomes clear how angry Mrs Johnson is with her husband. This has been going on for twenty years. They never actually got divorced, and now she still comes to visit him every day.

8 August – There has been a penetrating conversation between the head nurse and Mrs Johnson, followed by a conversation between her and the psychologist. Mrs Johnson appears to be extremely angry with her husband. She reported that her husband used to work as an auditor. He had always been extremely correct, not prepared to fiddle with what he found. He had no understanding for those with perspectives different from his own. He was not popular, and he was proud of that. 'Sometimes it is hard to have sympathy for that man,' one of the team members said.

20 August – Mr Johnson has passed away. His situation had slowly deteriorated. The team is still in touch with his wife, because his death has set free a lot of emotions in the family.

Mr Johnson's story helps us to see an important dimension of the theme that is central to this chapter: how hard it is to be honest to oneself and each other about the things in life that are bad or have failed. There is no doubt that the farewell ritual in the middle of June had been an authentic event for all who participated. But it could only have worked out well had Mr Johnson died shortly afterwards. For his wife, the ritual had a real liberation as final closure after twenty long years of being imprisoned in a difficult marriage. By closing it in harmony the relief that it was over would have overwhelmed her anger, remorse and sorrow. She had the inner space to walk the last mile upright before breaking down right after the finish. But then the finish did not come and she had to walk on for another two months. And this asked too much of her.

Had the farewell ritual been too superficially harmonious, covering up what was really going on? Had it failed because it had not been honest or thorough enough? Questions like these are hard to answer. In the new *ars moriendi* there is no other sharp criterion than the inner space present in all the people who participated in the ritual. From that perspective, it seems that the ritual had served the valuable purpose of expressing the importance of being together as a family at such a difficult moment in life. Sometimes rituals lead to unexpected processes of reconciliation, but these can never be planned or forced.

The question: 'How do I look back on my life' is connected with shame, hesitation and resistance for that part which is related to guilt and failure. It takes a lot of inner space to be able to be honest here, both to oneself and to other people. All of us want to be successful and happy, or at least believe and pretend that we are. Sensing the right moment to address issues that people deny or forget is one of the virtues that is needed in order to do well in this area. However, not everything that goes wrong in life can be understood in terms of causality or guilt. And Mr Johnson was an example of someone who was a difficult personality due to a mixture of character traits, psychiatric factors and the more or less free decisions he had made in life. This brings us to the subject of the last section of this chapter: the tragic.

The tragic

When discussing the polarity between doing and undergoing we saw that we live in a culture of action and control. When someone who has been a chain smoker for thirty years is diagnosed with lung cancer, we may feel that this is not surprising. People who do not smoke themselves might even think there is a certain reassurance in this, because it follows statistical probability. In the first chapter we suggested that this might be one of the tricks that death plays on us – to make us believe that a healthy lifestyle is rewarded by a long life. As long as the statistics are reliable, one can strive to remain on the right side of the line, and everything is under control.

What appears as action and control in the polarity between doing and undergoing presents itself as responsibility in the tension between forgiving and forgetting. Freedom and responsibility are the foundations of morality and they lead to the idea that acting well is rewarded by happiness and prosperity. Acting wrong or unjustly is followed by guilt and punishment. In the case of Mr Johnson and his family, however, we have seen that life is far more complex and unreliable. In life many things happen where it is hard to see clearly who was responsible for what. There are situations for which there is no clear solution or explanation. They are related to the vulnerability and unpredictability of our existence. The case of Mr Johnson appealed to our capacity to undergo and endure rather than our ability to do and act. It confronts us with the dimension of the tragic. Asking the question: 'How do I look back on my life' with inner space means looking at our life with a certain mildness and being open to the uncertainty, unfairness and incomprehensibility that is characteristic of the world as we know it. Our vulnerability as human beings confronts us with the 'fragility of goodness' (Nussbaum 1986). What does it mean for our struggle to make sense of our life and the bits and pieces that do not fit clear evaluation in terms of responsibility? Perhaps our confrontation with the tragic can teach us four things (Manschot 2003).

In the first place, the tragic asks us to be open to human reality as it presents itself. Before there can be any analysis or understanding of a situation, the tragic asks for openness and attentiveness – inner space which allows us to see that many people who are difficult or damaging to other people are often also victims themselves. This acceptance of reality as it presents itself to us, without judgement, helps us to understand a situation more deeply by connecting to the inner polyphony of ourselves and the people involved in the situation.

In the second place, the tragic reconfirms the importance of emotions in understanding a situation. When emotions are taken seriously, we open the way to our intuitions and the ambiguity of many situations. Emotions also connect us with the inner perspective of people and help us to understand their situation in a more existential way.

Because the tragic confronts us with the insecurity of human life, in the third place, it is important to be reliable and to give confidence. The older woman in Chapter 2 – the lady with the euthanasia declaration in her bag – could only deal with her situation in a new way from the moment she gained confidence that her physician was really concerned with her. From that moment on she understood that she did not have to take care of herself any longer, but could rely on a physician who would not leave her to her own devices.

For those who give formal or informal care, it means that they have to be open to risks and prepared to cross the boundaries between the professional and the private dimensions of life (Heijst 2011). Human action implies uncertainty and risks, and those who try to eliminate these two eliminate an important humane dimension in caring that is related to our freedom and originality as human beings. The question 'How do I look back on my life?' can only be answered well by compassionate ears and eyes and a compassionate presence.

8

What Can I Hope For?

One morning, after I had bathed Michael, I took care of his skin with oil. Gently rubbing the oil into his fragile skin, I asked him whether he had made up his mind about what to do if his situation suddenly turned so bad that it became unbearable.

'Yes,' he said, 'I have taken care of everything. They know exactly what to do. But the fear remains.'

'Fear of what?' I asked. 'Fear of the pain or of what comes after?'

'Not of the pain,' he replied. 'They will make sure that I will feel no pain anymore. But no one knows what comes after. Nobody has ever proven that there will be anything after.'

'But no one has proven that there is nothing after either,' I tried.

'You are right,' he said, 'but if there would be anything after, then billions of people would be somewhere. And the world is overpopulated already.'

'Some people nevertheless have confidence that something good will happen after death,' I replied.

He smiled: 'Yeah, well, I am not prepared for it. It just isn't my time yet. I am not ready for it.'

Of course, I thought, can any young father in his early thirties be ready for death, having two little children and so many loose ends?

Looking back on this conversation many years later, I cannot be but embarrassed by my part of it. I had not really listened to Michael. I had not asked him about his fear. I had awkwardly proposed to him views that other people have about the unanswerable question of what comes after this life. And he had made it very clear, by expressing the same sentiment in three different phrases, that he was not ready to go yet. Could I have done better? Could the new *ars moriendi* have helped me here?

I think the new *ars moriendi* could have helped me here very well indeed; in the first place by distinguishing between the content of what someone thinks – this is the level on which I tried to answer his thoughts – and the underlying foundation of this content: the kind of knowledge that is helpful for him in answering unanswerable questions. For the big questions in life, North Atlantic culture does not have one single framework that is shared by everyone. To the contrary, there are many diferent views about God, death and afterlife. For our new *ars moriendi* more important than the great variety of views is the logic underlying it. Before we come to explaining this logic, let us first take a look at the direction in which contemporary society leads us.

A disenchanted society

As we have sketched in earlier chapters, the culture we live in is characterized by a strong belief in rationality. We are still children of the Enlightenment, that movement in the eighteenth century that deeply influenced the way we looked at reality. By the sixteenth and seventeenth centuries there had already been an empirical turn in our approach to the world. These are the centuries in which the foundations of contemporary medicine were laid. Medical knowledge was no longer handed down by copying books of great authorities, but new knowledge was created by a combination of experiments and logical thinking. A great number of discoveries by people like Nicolaus Copernicus and Isaac Newton had strengthened the idea that the structure of reality could be understood by using empirical experiments, logic and mathematics. By understanding reality, it could be controlled and manipulated.

One of the central features of Modernity, as the great cultural transformation after the Middle Ages is also called, is the rejection of tradition and authority. New foundations of knowledge were sought, based on rationality. This concerned even the areas that were traditionally the domain of the churches: metaphysics and morality. Immanuel Kant's deep reflections on the foundations of knowledge and morality have deeply influenced our culture. And David Hume's ideas about the foundation of morality on an empirical basis are perhaps even more influential in the way most of us look at ethics. Although deeply disagreeing about the limits of human thinking and whether rational knowledge or empirical knowledge should be the foundation of our world view, both thinkers agreed on the rejection of tradition and authority as a foundation of ethics.

Once the foundations of modern thinking were laid down, in the nineteenth and twentieth centuries the work of Darwin, Marx and Freud further broke down the illusions about the superior status of humanity.

The development of hermeneutics after Schleiermacher paved the way for the crisis of meaning in postmodernism, and the great massacres of the twentieth century showed that rationality and technology could also turn against humaneness. The era in which we live now – there is dispute as to whether we should call it late-, post-, liquid- or high-Modernity – is characterized by disenchantment and fragmentation of knowledge.

The disenchantment of the world is visible in the marginalization of institutionalized religion in the North Atlantic world. Although this process takes different forms in different countries, what they all have in common is that religious authority is waning. Apart from minorities that cling to fundamentalism or traditionalism, the majority of the population shows an ongoing decline in traditional beliefs about a personal God and an afterlife. The need for rational arguments and empirical evidence has replaced confidence and trust in the wisdom of old institutions. Press coverage of financial and sexual scandals has even further proven the fallibility of these institutions. Many people have left and are leaving the churches for these reasons. But the process is also visible inside institutionalized religion, where a more secular approach to morality and metaphysics has replaced the traditional sense of the sacred.

The fragmentation of knowledge is experienced in many areas and on many levels. In medicine the amount of knowledge produced has led to an ongoing process of specialization. People know more about less, and it becomes harder to keep the greater picture in view. On a practical level this leads to patients being reduced to organs and a failure to treat the person as a whole. On the scientific level this has led to the rise of evidence-based medicine that seeks to manage the excess of information by reducing it radically according to strict standards before combining it with clinical experience and patients' values. Evidence-based medicine is paralleled by a number of other developments that aim to reduce complexity and increase fragmentation.

What is the impact of these greater developments on the cultural context in which patients ask themselves the metaphysical question: 'What can I hope for?' First, we see that the question of hope is interpreted as a request for information rather than a request for inspiration. Hope is interpreted as knowledge about the future, and when knowledge is based on measuring, the question of hope is interpreted as a question of realistic prognosis. We will come back to this in more detail later in this chapter.

Second, within this framework a shift also takes place in the appreciation of the spiritual and religious dimension of our existence. These two dimensions are seen as possibly functional within the framework of a disenchanted and rational world view. When spiritual belief in an afterlife gives someone the power to deal with a situation and reduce the experience of pain, it is functional and can be used effectively. As a coping strategy it becomes part of a medical way of framing reality, as opposed to how the insider perspective of spirituality and religion works: as an overarching horizon of meaning.

Third, in a culture sceptical about authority no one is denied the freedom of soul-searching and expressing this in their own unique way. To a certain degree this is even stimulated and commercially exploited by a great variety of books, courses, techniques, or practices related to healthy behaviour, ecological sustainability and global justice. What is radically different from preceding centuries is that spirituality and religion are no longer connected to a shared horizon; both are privatized and individualized. What people hope for or believe in is their personal and private decision. In some countries, healthcare professionals are even reluctant to ask about it for this reason. One's spirituality is seen as a part of one's intimate realm, completely subjective, not to be criticized and thus outside the realm of morality.

Knowing and believing

In my conversation with Michael I did not succeed in connecting with his concerns because I answered him at a superficial level of things people believe in, instead of listening to where and how he was searching for solid ground to answer the big question: 'What can I hope for?' To what extent can the new *ars moriendi* help here, allowing Michael to be listened to in such a way that he might experience more inner space?

The way in which people look for solid ground for metaphysical questions in the disenchanted society described above can be presented on a continuum ranging from knowing on the one hand, and believing on the other. Again, we will see that the positions on this continuum have a different character, depending on how much inner space there is. The more people cling to one extreme, the more fixed people are in the way they look for something to hold on to. Because knowing and believing are concepts that can have different meanings, depending on the context in which they are used, I will define them in a specific way.

The pole of knowing is defined here as the position in which solid ground is sought in a specific form of knowledge – empirically based rational knowledge. In terms of new forms of authority, for many people who reject religious views, science plays the new role of provider of reliable information. According to science, the brain will stop functioning when it has been cut off from oxygen for more than a couple of minutes. Since we can only experience things as long as our brain functions, we can be sure that after dying we will not experience anything anymore.

This view on the impossibility of an afterlife is widespread. It is considered to be a rational and empirically based position. But it can be held in different forms depending on how much inner space people have. If there is no inner space at all, people will cling to this position and refuse any discussion about it. To them, this position is the only possible rational view and it is important to defend it in order to have a hold amid the uncertainty of metaphysical questions.

One might, however, question whether this position is a scientific one itself. Science can only progress if there is a fundamental openness to new insights. In order to maintain this openness, any theory about reality is just what it is: a human and fallible hypothesis about a part of reality that is represented in a model based on complexity reduction. Within the theoretical framework in which the model is formulated, everything may be rationally clear and convincing. But science becomes really exciting when phenomena are encountered that cannot be explained by the dominant theoretical framework. Then either the phenomena should be denied, or the theoretical framework should be revised.

An interesting example of this is the research of the Dutch cardiologist Pim van Lommel, who interviewed 344 cardiac patients who were successfully resuscitated after cardiac arrest in ten Dutch hospitals (Lommel *et al.* 2001). Of these patients, eighteen per cent reported a near death experience. With the current scientific consensus about the brain producing information, van Lommel could not explain his findings. In his later work, therefore, he developed an alternative explanation of near death experiences, according to which the brain is the receiver of information, rather than producing it. Van Lommel was severely criticized by many of his colleagues for leaving the dominant framework of explanation, but one cannot deny that his attitude is scientific in its open mindedness.

The openness of van Lommel's position is based on the recognition that scientific explanations are fallible because they are principally reductionist. With regard to metaphysical questions, this may generate an open attitude towards other sources of knowledge that are of a different nature from rational knowledge. For this reason, van Lommel is, for example, open to art and spiritual traditions in other cultures where he finds information that is in accordance with his findings.

The acknowledgement of the limitations of the scientific paradigm (which is an indication of inner space), however, can also result in the position of denying the possibility of gaining any reliable knowledge beyond the boundaries of science. This position with regard to metaphysical issues can be called agnostic. People who hold this position have a certain openness, stating that it is impossible to know for certain anything beyond the boundaries of sciences. Religion may be right about what happens after death; however, the problem is that we cannot prove it.

Interestingly, at the other side of the spectrum, the most extreme form of believing relates very well to this position of agnosticism. According to traditional Judaism, Christianity and Islam, for example, faith is adherence to what cannot be proven by science; and precisely because it cannot be proven by science God has helped humankind with additional knowledge based on divine revelation.

Again we see that both poles of the continuum between knowing and believing can exclude each other when they are defined in a specific way.

In its most extreme form, at the pole of believing we find the position which is called fideism, which states that faith is independent of and superior to reason. This position can be connected with different authorities and more or less inner space. One extreme form, for example, is fundamentalism that holds 'literal' interpretation of holy texts as the foundation of a particular faith. In this position there is no inner space that allows for other interpretations or the idea of religion as historically developing. There is also no possible other source that may challenge the unique interpretation that is the right one. Any deviation of this interpretation is considered to be a deviation of faith.

But there are more positions possible at the pole of believing. There is also a position that is more subjectivist and based on personal experiences. In line with the pole of forgetting, we described in the previous chapter that what one believes is the authentic and unique answer to the experiences one has had. In this position there is more inner space than we will find in the case of the fundamentalist one: one's subjective belief can develop and grow, deepening new experiences and discovering new dimensions. This position is more in line with the logic of the acorn, whereas the fundamentalist would rather adhere to the road map.

Considering versions of both poles with less and more inner space, again we see that the more inner space there is, the more integration or polyphony of the various positions is possible. It is indeed possible to have as a foundation of one's world view a combination of elements that are derived from science, spiritual traditions and one's own experiences. These can be integrated into a personal world view, but they can also be existing parallel to each other and simultaneously.

The position with the maximum of inner space is perhaps the radical position that is not in need of any solid foundation in metaphysical matters. It may well be, however, that in those cases a solid foundation where one is able to live with unanswered questions is found elsewhere. When I was 15 years old, I remember asking the local parish priest whether he would be disappointed if when walking through the heavenly gates he would discover that there was no God, but a big smiling Buddha would welcome him. The priest laughed and said: 'Not at all. I live a life that I consider valuable and I enjoy living it every day. I do not think about what comes after my death. I like to be surprised.'

Inner space

Michael was not afraid to die. He was afraid of what comes after because he did not know what to think of it. If we interpret his position against the background of the polarity of knowing and believing, he seemed to be stuck in a one-way street around the pole of knowing. His rational thinking told him that it was impossible that there was anything after death. But he did not seem to be completely satisfied with this conclusion. His rational thinking did not help him any further and he did not know how to proceed differently. In his view the only alternative option would be to believe, but he did not consider himself to be a religious person.

Thinking back of Michael's position, I recognize the position of many people who find themselves helpless in front of the big questions in life. Science doesn't help, religion is no option, and how to find a third way – or a different perspective on the issue – is a mystery to them. In the new *ars moriendi* we propose to support people by focusing on the development of inner space. This inner space can be found by listening to our inner polyphony and discovering the space between the many voices that are part of who we are.

We will explore the inner polyphony in two steps. First we will discuss four meanings of death that we often find in our culture, and see what inner space can achieve with regard to each of the four meanings. Subsequently, we will focus on our inner polyphony with regard to the concept of hope, which is both a central concept at the end of life and part of the central question of this chapter. But let us first hear from four people working at the palliative care unit, who formulated different views on the question of how they looked at death and what their patients could hope for.

> I have had a religious education, but I never go to church. I have a kind of confidence that there is something out there and that there is a life after death. But how exactly, I do not know. I don't have to know everything. It is okay the way it is. (Psychologist, 32 years old)

> Where will you be after you die? Fertilizer for the plants! I do believe that the spirit of a person can stay with you. At the moment of dying everything is not gone at once. There is time needed to say goodbye, to process it. There is still a kind of presence then. (Nurse, 29 years old)

> Death is terrible, saying goodbye to people you love. Nevertheless I can see that it is part of life and a solution for people who become a wreck and waste away.

I do not believe in God: one cannot imagine what that could be. Still I am almost convinced that there is something: everything is made so ingeniously. There must be something for all the people who have lived. It cannot be over just like that. (Head nurse, 53 years old)

Of course, I am confronted with death a lot. I am consciously at pains not to consider it routine. That would be wrong. I must say that my view on death has changed. It is not a loaded topic anymore. I can speak to a family and be relaxed. Death is inherent to life. And still death remains wondrous. I was born and raised on a farm and I see a great similarity with birth, for example stopping breathing versus beginning to breathe. After death something else begins. (Physician, 35 years old)

Death has many faces and meanings. As we read these views of people who work professionally in a nursing home and are regularly confronted with death, it appears that they all have an inner polyphony. They do not consider themselves to be religious or churchgoing, but their views reflect fragments of the traditional Christian narrative. Discovering the inner polyphony of different faces or meanings of death being present simultaneously can be helpful in creating inner space in two ways.

In the first place, acknowledging and accepting that different meanings of death are simultaneously playing a role in one's experience can give cognitive space in the sense of opening up different perspectives and emotional space, accepting that one is torn by or divided between different emotions and feelings. In the second place, each one of these faces of death can also have different meanings that create an inner polyphony of their own. Discovering this inner polyphony can also create space in offering new perspectives on the reality of what one is experiencing.

Let us take a closer look at three basic meanings of death, open to whatever position on the continuum of knowing and believing that is present in the four quotes above and see to what extent the recognition of the polyphony can help to create inner space and bring comfort.

A first face of death, related to the human life cycle, is death as a natural end of life. All that lives is born to die. Or as Benjamin Franklin framed it in 1789 in a letter to Jean-Baptiste Leroy: 'In this world nothing can be said to be certain except death and taxes.' This one view of death, as an inevitable fate of all human beings, can have many meanings: it can be seen as evidence for the hopelessness, absurdity and futility of human life; it may provide great consolation in the thought that to all suffering there comes an end; it may make us aware of our connectedness with all other living creatures that have the same destiny; it may make us aware of the unique possibilities and importance of every moment we have in our lives.

Every one of these meanings can be explored separately and all of them offer possibilities for creating inner space. In realizing that we are connected with all other living creatures, for example, we may see that there is no need to fear something as natural as dying. Billions of people have done it before, and billions will do it after we have died. In our solidarity with other human beings, we may be able to position ourselves in the bigger picture of humanity. This solidarity may help to loosen the ties of our self-centredness and our inclination to cling to the preservation of ourselves, whatever the costs are.

A second face of death, related to the social nature of human beings, is death as a destroyer of bonds, traditionally represented as the grim reaper, who cuts off the relations between the living and the dead. He cuts off lives without discrimination, and is the greatest enemy one can think of, taking away even the people we love the most. It is clear that this face of death – strongly related to the polarity of holding on and letting go – is often so dominant that it pushes away all other meanings of death. Again, however, this face of death has many meanings: it can be seen as the final argument as to why one should never fall in love and attach to anyone; it can be a great liberator in the case of bad relationships, giving those who are left behind a second chance in life; it can be a source of guilt with regard to everything one had wanted to say or do to someone; it can be seen as a great source of fear to lose the ones that are most dear.

Inner space cannot help in preventing the future loss of lost ones, but it can redirect the attention to the here and now. One of the experiences often heard around a deathbed is that people hugely value that time because of the much more intensive communication that characterizes that period. Sometimes these months or weeks are seen as the most valuable in a long-term relationship, a period that they would never have wanted to miss. Because we suddenly realize the uniqueness of every day, every moment, we are confronted with the value of the time that we can share with our loved ones. Realizing this can bring mildness and inner space, allowing us to really live the moments we can share with each other. Having lived life together to its full extent we will still be sad, but not be left behind with the feeling that – as John Lennon sings in the song 'Beautiful Boy' – 'Life is what happens when you're making other plans.'

A third face of death, related to the limits of human knowledge, is that of the great unknown. Every idea about being dead or what happens after death is based on what we know as living human beings. The great variety of viewpoints that are possible with regard to death as the door to the great unknown have already been discussed when presenting the various positions on the continuum between the poles of knowing and believing. They can be a source of comfort and of fear, as in the case of Michael. All of these positions can be experienced with more or less inner space.

Nevertheless, accepting death as a limit to human knowledge can be a source of further inner space when one has developed the inner space of living with questions that are unanswered. Living with unanswered questions can be the result of being not interested, but that is not what is meant here. The position meant here is the generous position in which one does not have the urge to push or cross limits, but can live with the radical otherness of death. By not projecting new meanings in the black hole of death, or imagining a beautiful next stage behind the curtains, we can humbly and generously accept the limits of our knowledge.

The many faces of death and their subsequent polyphony of meanings can be confusing, liberating, puzzling, or seen as a way in which death continues to play tricks on us. In the new *ars moriendi* the directedness is not towards highlighting specific meanings and suppressing other meanings, as was the case in the medieval *ars moriendi*. Having inner space as its foundation and objective, it aims to help us accept our inner polyphony and discover which voices can be a point of departure for developing more inner space to cope with the paradoxes and tensions of life and death.

The many faces of death and their meanings impact on the question: 'What can I hope for?' But hope itself is also a complex phenomenon. Therefore we will turn now to the polyphony of hope.

The polyphony of hope

Hope is an important force in human life that connects us with the future. Hope keeps people going, it is an important element of well-being and has a positive effect on recovery. But what if there is no recovery and there seems to be no future to be connected to? Isn't the question: 'What can I hope for?' a particularly cruel one in the new *ars moriendi*? Shouldn't we rather focus on the opposite of hope in the case of terminally ill patients?

When we ask for the opposite of hope, interestingly there are two candidates that are of a completely different nature and opposed to each other in their turn (Kylmä and Vehviläinen-Julkunen 1997). The first opposite of hope is hopelessness. In the same way as hope is a force with energy and vitality which connects us with things in the future that are hard or seemingly impossible to reach, hopelessness is the loss of this energy and vitality, submerging us in an atmosphere of apathy. Opposed to apathy, and the second opposite of hope, is the force that is called despair. In the case of despair, we are convinced that the goal that we had hoped for cannot be reached, but we are still in possession of the energy and vitality that directs us towards the future. Despair is the force that seeks other solutions or new objects in the future to connect with.

Contrary to hopelessness and despair, hope is a force which is connected with inner space. As long there is hope, there is room for a different future to the one that is expected or likely to come according to prognosis. Hope is related to faith, as it is able to build on what is not evident or visible. It is connected with creativity and fantasy because it is connected with a strong desire to reach a certain end or object. In its creativeness, hope is hard to grasp and is a force that keeps life going in the direction of an imagined future.

Hope is conceptualized and approached differently in different disciplines. According to an analysis of the literature on hope in palliative care, there are roughly speaking three ways in which professional caregivers approach hope (Olsman *et al.* 2014). The most usual perspective used by physicians is to look at the hope that patients have against the background of asking whether this hope is realistic. Hope is measured against prognosis, and when hope is more positive than the prognosis it is called unrealistic. In that case they see it as their moral duty to inform patients honestly so that they may adjust their hope to reality. The medical prognosis is seen as the most reliable access to true knowledge and leaving a patient with false hope is considered equal to deceit or telling a lie. Only when the hope of patients is realistic can they begin to make plans and anticipate the future.

Although this approach to hope is important and the most common one in medical literature – often related to medical ethical questions about truth-telling – it also brings a problem with it. Apart from the fact that hope measured against prognosis is often connected with calculations of probability that are hard for patients to understand, hope is also a vital force that helps people to deal with their situation. In some Mediterranean cultures, for example, it is important never to give up hope and to make sure that the patients remain connected to this force of life. This connectedness is more important than the information about prognostic probabilities.

The second perspective we find in healthcare is that of hope as a coping mechanism. In this perspective the force of hope is acknowledged fully, and the most important thing is that the hope of patients is supported so that they are better able to carry their disease. This perspective, understanding hope from a psychosocial angle, is often found in the work of psychologists and social workers. Hope is seen as a functional force that is helpful. Whether this hope is realistic is an important question, but not the first and most vital question. More important is the question of how people are able to live with their uncertain future, bear the treatments they have to undergo and experience a certain quality of life.

The third perspective of hope is even less interested in its relation to any realistic prognosis. Here hope is seen as a way of experiencing meaning and sense in a certain situation. This perspective could be called the narrative perspective, because hope is first and foremost interpreted within the framework of one's life story. It is found in the work of chaplains and psychologists. Facing one's own death one is forced to write the final chapter to one's life story, as we have seen in Chapter 4. People make sense of what happens to them by placing it in a meaningful and coherent order that is connected to the way they see themselves. Such a meaningful order is a story developing in time and comprising past, present and future. This meaning always has a dimension open to the future, which has value on its own, whether it is realistic or not.

Many patients who are terminally ill know very well that they will not live until, for example, the next football championship, like Mr McNeal in Chapter 5. Still they might want to focus on that perspective or even start something they will never be able to finish like a Spanish course or listening to the complete works of Bach. From the realistic perspective one might suspect that what they call hope is actually a form of denial. From the narrative perspective, however, these initiatives rather appear as acts though which patients express that they are still connected with life or with things that are highly meaningful to them. These actions have a value of their own. From the functional perspective one could say that the importance of these actions is that they make sure that patients are able to cope with their situation and carry on.

The three perspectives of hope can be used separately or in combination with one another. Sometimes they overlap. In communication with patients one can try to attune to their actual needs by choosing the perspective that is the most appropriate to their concerns. Departing from this, one may explore the other two perspectives. In North Atlantic culture the perspective on hope as something that needs to be adjusted to realistic prognosis is dominant and close to the pole of knowing. The other two perspectives are closer to the pole of believing. Only with inner space is one able to bridge the distance between the two approaches.

When we approach the question: 'What can I hope for?' with inner space, within the continuum of knowing and believing, being aware of the many faces of death and their meanings and the conceptualizations of hope, we create a space for exploring and building a meaningful perspective at the end of life. The inner polyphony of patients will vary over time and resembles a singing choir in which voices are harmonizing, alternating or moving from the foreground to the background (Olsman *et al.* 2015). But that richness may well be an advantage when searching for themes that help to develop inner space.

9

The *Ars Moriendi* Model
in Religious Perspective

The new *ars moriendi* has been developed in order
to offer a spiritual framework, integrated in the
interdisciplinary approach of palliative care, open to anyone
who wishes to reflect on the important questions at the end
of life. Since many people view their spirituality in a religious
way, the new *ars moriendi* would be a failure if it were not
open to that option. In this chapter, therefore, we will
review the preceding chapters from a religious perspective.
We will discover that in this review the structure of the *ars
moriendi* remains the same but some fundamental changes
will occur in the way the model functions.

Since there is no abstract religious perspective, only a
multitude of perspectives from specific religious traditions,
in this chapter I will limit my perspective to one specific
tradition. The religious perspective I will develop can be
situated within the Roman Catholic tradition. However,
as there is great diversity among the 1.27 billion people
who belong to that tradition in how and what they believe,
this chapter should be read as one particular version of
Roman Catholicism.

The reason I limit myself to the Roman Catholic
tradition is because it is the only religious tradition I know

from the inside. I was born and raised in that tradition (or at least the Dutch version of it) and have studied its theology for many years. This enables me to write from an insider's perspective and stay close to a lived spirituality. Other users of the *ars moriendi* might develop a different view from their own spiritual tradition.

Why is it so important to write from an insider's perspective? Because one cannot really understand what it means to be religious from an outsider's perspective. Being religious is like being in a loving relationship. Many aspects of it are only understandable by living it. The real value of it can only be experienced from the lived engagement that is born from a will to believe in someone. And vice versa: the experience of being loved by someone opens up a new perspective on both one's partner and oneself.

Let us now look at the five central questions of the *ars moriendi* and see how they sound from a religious perspective, sometimes resonating with other questions, sometimes extending the question, sometimes reframing the question, but never leaving the framework consisting of the five polarities.

Who am I and what do I really want?

As we developed a framework for reflecting on human identity and autonomy we identified three fundamental relationships that could be situated in a dialectic relation between the poles of myself and the others. There is no direct access to the self, but we discover who we are and what we really want via the relationship between me and myself, me and my fellow human beings, and me and the institutional dimension of my life. From a religious perspective one new relationship is added that has a great impact on the existing three: the relationship with God. This relationship does not compromise autonomy, but presents itself as a horizon by which everything is put into a new perspective.

God has many faces, and there is hardly a word that evokes reactions that are more controversial. In this chapter I will use the word God for a 'personal mystery of love'. Let me clarify the three elements of this phrase. First, God is not approached as an abstract or faceless power of love but as a personal God with whom one can enter into a relationship. Second, although in this personal relationship one can get to know God better, he will never be known in the way creatures know other creatures: God remains an incomprehensible mystery beyond what can be thought or expressed by created language (Sokolowksi 1982). And third, God is creative love wanting everything created to share in his creative love.

If we focus on the relation between me and myself, two fundamental changes are caused by the relationship with God. In the first place, one's life story is embedded in a larger story: the story of God with humanity, of which the apostolic creed can be seen as the theological abstract. In this larger framework my life story receives a new beginning and a new ending. Being involved in God's mystery of love, being invited to actively and consciously participate in this creative process of God, means that I am loved as a child of God from the beginning, no matter how difficult my situation on earth is. And at the end of my life I may entrust myself into the loving hands of God, in the confidence that he will take care of me and know what to do with what remains of me.

In the second place, apart from becoming part of a bigger story and a destination for life, within this dimension something else happens as well. With the eyes of faith I will discover that it is not me who writes the story of my life all by myself, but that someone bigger than me is holding my pen. I am invited to be co-author and write my story as a personal version of a universal story. My life story is intertextually related to the life story of Jesus of Nazareth – the unique human being in whom God has revealed himself in terms of humaneness for once and for all – and every saint who has lived ever after. My life story is a unique version of the universal story of every human being who discovers himself to be in a loving relationship with God.

Also in the interpersonal dimension, two important changes take place. First, a new interpersonal relation is added to my life. The daily conversation with God makes my life a life in continuous dialogue, even before any other human being enters the scene. This dialogue shapes the self through the practice of daily prayer. Prayer helps to enlarge my inner space and to redirect my life to the divine secret of love. Prayer is a continuous exercise in the desire to be united with God's love, in this earthly life and after this life.

The second fundamental change regards the relation with my fellow human beings. The central prayer of the Christian tradition is the Our Father. By saying the words of this prayer reality is reframed, by calling God 'Father' I become a child of God, and all fellow human beings – being children of the same Father – become brothers and sisters. A lifelong moral programme is hidden in this one short prayer.

The institutional dimension – the Catholic Church as a community of faith – is also of crucial importance for the relationship with God. We do not have direct access to God as a mystery of love. Just as is the case with the human self, we only have access indirectly, via the stories, rituals, texts and prayers. In this process of tradition, people from all ages and places play a role and together they offer the keys for reading reality in the light of faith and discovering God's presence in reality. By being baptized I am being reborn and my identity is reframed by another dimension that I do not own but that calls me.

The institutional dimension thus is the foundation for the changes in the personal and the interpersonal dimension. At the same time, this institutional dimension might be the hardest to accept. As an organization of sinners the Catholic Church is no better than any other human organization, and the fact that the Catholic Church considers itself God-given does not prevent it from keeping God's goodness out of sight from time to time.

What does all this mean for human autonomy? In the light of faith the self appears as a self in conversation with God. That self is as free as any other self, and when it follows what it believes to be the will of God, it does so out of a free choice to subject one's will to a larger goodness ('thy will be done'). Any choices and decisions in this area are based on a dialectical process in which, again, inner space plays a central role.

How do I deal with suffering?

When the interviewer asks what having this painful bone disease has meant for her religious life, Hannemieke Stamperius, in the same interview from which the previous quotes in Chapter 5 are taken, answers (Stamperius 2009):

> I was raised Dutch reformed and a large part of my life I have been a convinced atheist. When I was diagnosed with this bone disease, it happened to be around Easter. I saw that man hanging on that cross again and suddenly realized that pain is central to Christianity.

And that from this one can learn how soul and body can be in harmony with each other. From then on I started to pore over theology. It is a brilliant discipline: the centre of all questions, God, will always remain a great unknown. That makes me cheerful: that you will not get an answer to all those big questions. I have started to believe and I see that as a jump from my pain to that of the world. If you do not accept pain, you are forlorn, grumpy and nobody understands you. If you do accept it, you are extremely close to the sorrow of others. (Translation: Carlo Leget)

These words summarize a long process of discovery through lived experience. What is formulated here is in essence exactly what Pope John Paul II said in his apostolic letter *Salvifici doloris* (1984). Having survived an attack in May 1981, the Pope meditated on human suffering during his recovery, resulting in his theological letter. What is special about this document is the fact that suffering is approached as a mystery and all answers to the question of suffering are insufficient. The letter is written in such a way that the reader is invited to follow a process of searching for answers. It starts with a journey through both testaments of the Christian Bible, and concludes with saying that there is no other way of discovering the 'salvific meaning of suffering' (which is also the title of the letter) than to go down that road oneself. In the lived confrontation with suffering one may understand the meaning of suffering, and the more one opens up to the suffering of other people, the more one discovers the meaning of one's own suffering. The suffering of Christ can play a central role in this, for he opened up a space in which people can connect their suffering with the suffering of other people in a process of transforming suffering into love.

Writing about suffering needs an insider's perspective in order to be solidly grounded in the experiences of real people. Otherwise the same may happen as what happens when we start to think about death: suffering may play many tricks on us. The extent to which being connected with the suffering of Christ might be comforting in real life is very well expressed in a story that a friend of mine told me who was a parish priest at the time. He was called to visit an old farmer who was dying. Being a simple and faithful man the farmer had great trouble communicating with his children who were not connected with or inspired by the Church anymore. As he suffered from breathlessness one of his sons cynically remarked: 'Well Dad, so much for your faith in Jesus Christ. He isn't really a great help now you are dying, is he?' The old man calmly looked at his son and replied: 'He is a greater help than you are at this moment, for he has already experienced it all.'

Considering the poles of doing and undergoing from the perspective of the Christian tradition, this tradition offers many possible ways of connecting to the central mystery of suffering transformed into love. Although faith is an act, a practice and a virtue that is associated with being open, receptive and passive, at the same time it is clear that the dialectical process of being connected with God also implies a lot of activity and doing. Again, both poles of the dialectical process are involved here.

If we finally reflect on the role of inner space, one might say that inner space is recognized here as the readiness of discovering new things that one had never taken for being possible. Hannemieke Stamperius reports that she has been a convinced atheist for most of her adult life. Rediscovering the wisdom of the religious tradition of her youth takes an openness and courage that is a great blessing in her case.

How can I say goodbye?

Religious faith is full of holding on and letting go. Believing in God, trusting and loving God is holding on to a divine mystery of love, a God who is almost incomprehensible, and whom we believe holds us in his hands. At the same time, believing in God is letting go of all ideas about God that might stand in the way of encountering the real divine presence. It is taking up and holding on to the responsibility of leading one's life as one thinks God has meant it to be, and simultaneously letting go of any expectation of a good result or a reward.

The dialectic of holding on and letting go is practised in many ways in Christian spirituality. As a preparation for the great feasts of Christmas and Easter, for example, there is a period of abstinence and purification. During Lent people abstain from the good things in life, training themselves to let go of them, or hold on to them with more inner space.

The most radical form of letting go as a religious attitude of life is shown by people who devote their life to God by abstaining from their freedom of will (obedience), earthly possessions (poverty) and sexual relations (chastity). Living such a life in which one lets go of the things that most people think are essential and indispensable to human happiness can only be successful and fulfilling when it is based on an authentic vocation.

As we have seen above with regard to the human self, being a Christian can be a lifelong journey of transformation. Our relationship with God as a heavenly Father transforms me into a child of God, and all fellow human beings appear as brothers and sisters. I am being connected with myself and my neighbours in a new way: through the relationship with God. When this relationship with God becomes the new centre of my life, this is the thing I should hold on to on any account.

In medieval theology this was expressed in the idea of the right order of love (Aquinas). First of all, I should love God above all other things in life, but also in all other things in life. My love of God should be the hidden motive in all my actions and the way I treat myself, my fellow human beings and all other creatures. Second, I should love and hold on to my own soul, my good relationship with God that is the most important centre of my life, since it connects me with my destination as a human being, in this earthly life or in the next life in heaven. Third, I should love the souls of my neighbours and help them to find their destination. No action of mine should disturb or endanger their relationship with God. And I should even be prepared to risk my life for the benefit of the faith of my neighbours. Last, I should love my own body; I should take care of it and respect it as sustaining the gift of life, but realizing that it is only a temporary vessel for something far more important and eternal: the relationship with God.

This order of love may be helpful in creating space for the process of saying goodbye that is part of the process of dying. In a Christian perspective, all earthly possessions are on loan and always of a temporary character. This is what the periods (or religious lifestyles) of abstinence teach us. The same goes for the human body. One can let go of the body, knowing that one should hold on to God who will know what to do with us after we have died.

With regard to our loved ones, the relationship with God can be seen as the eternal and imperishable connection with a reality beyond life and death. Believing is holding on to that reality and the confidence that through this connection there will somehow be a continuing bond with our loved ones. This does not mean, of course, that letting go of life from a Christian perspective isn't hard or sad. The pain of leaving people behind, or living with a loss, is as great as ever. But next to this pain there may be a connectedness that can bring spiritual consolation.

The more one can experience one's life as a spiritual journey of transformation into a closer connectedness with God, the more one is able to let go of life and surrender oneself to this great mystery of love.

How do I look back on my life?

Although we have approached God as the encompassing mystery of love, the Christian tradition has a deep sense that there is no cheap way of making right what has been done wrong against other people. This is impossible because of the dynamism of decentring of the self that we have described above. Those who live from the central relationship with God live from a centre outside themselves. From that perspective one is not primarily caring for one's own business. Those who use other people – either to have a life of privileged irresponsibility or to become a saint in heaven – haven't understood what Christian spirituality is about.

If one is not primarily concerned with one's own business, two things happen in relation to one's own shortcomings or mistakes. In the first place, it is easier to admit them. One's primary concern is not to look good in the eyes of other people or to cover up one's shortcomings. The primary concern is to be good in the eyes of God, for whom nothing is concealed. You can fool yourself but you cannot fool God. One's primary concern is that the mystery of love is reflected in one's comings and goings.

In the second place, the love for other people – connected with the love of God – ignites a desire to make right what has gone wrong. Real love and friendship are recognized by a tendency toward restoring relationships and repairing the life-sustaining network of human relations that makes this world a good place. This idea is behind the traditional idea of a purgatory after death in which the souls wanted to purify themselves before appearing to God: a self-wanted and self-inflicted period of cleansing.

When dealing with guilt and collecting power and courage in the last phase of life, rituals can play an important role. The story of the psalm of protest that was read aloud in order to give words to the struggle of the old man in Chapter 7 showed how surprisingly beneficial a farewell ritual at the end of life may be. In the Roman Catholic tradition there are – next to a number of rituals – three sacraments that can play a role at the end of life.

Sacraments are rituals, practices in which the relationship with God is expressed. At the same time, sacraments are more than rituals. In the Roman Catholic tradition there is a belief that although sacraments are performed and received by human beings, at the same time God is working as the encompassing mystery of love. At important moments in human life, sacraments draw people into the bigger story of God and humanity. This is also the case when the end of life comes near. Sacraments connect the visible with the invisible, they have an element of remembering – they are connected to the life of Christ – and an element of forgetting – they connect with God and make a new start in life.

First, there is the sacrament of Reconciliation. This sacrament can only work when one really feels sorry about what one has done, and there is an authentic desire to restore the right order between oneself and other people, between oneself and God. What has gone wrong should be confessed – remembered – in order to acknowledge that the feelings of guilt are based on real guilt. Consequently, a work of repair can be determined and one's sins can be forgiven – forgotten – so that one can let go of what is painful in the past.

Second, there is the sacrament of Anointing of the Sick. This (formerly known as Extreme Unction) consists of anointing one's hands and head. It can be requested by anyone who is ill in order to be healed or strengthened to bear one's situation and to be connected with God. But this sacrament can also be the place to connect one's own suffering with the bigger story of redemptive suffering in the world, as we discussed above in relation to the letter *Salvifici doloris*.

The third sacrament that can play a role is the Eucharist. In this, Christ's last supper on earth is represented, and taking part in the Eucharist is taking part in the healing power of this event. Bread and wine as corporeal food are symbolic of the spiritual food that one receives by being connected with God. Traditionally the last bread – the host – one received was called 'food for on the road' or *viaticum*, which corresponds to the image of life on earth as a journey towards one's eternal destination.

Sacraments help people to reconnect with God, the centre of love from which they live and die. With regard to the question: 'How do I look back on my life', an important shift takes place. For when the self is decentred, this question is also rephrased into: 'How does God look back on my life?' And this is exactly what is expressed in the idea of the Last Judgement. I may have many ideas about how good or bad my life was, but I can never have an overview of all the consequences of my deeds, good and bad. Only God knows, and only God can make the final judgement. This brings us to the last question of the new *ars moriendi*.

What can I hope for?

The question: 'What can I hope for?' has been discussed within the dialectical framework of knowing and believing. If we reconsider the tension between knowing and believing from a religious perspective, doesn't that necessarily lead us to giving up the tension and focusing on belief alone?

As we have seen in the previous chapter, a position inspired by the pole of believing does not necessarily exclude a relation to knowing. Nevertheless, a religious point of view does have a great impact on both poles. Faith can be connected with inner space to the extent that it opens up reality as possibly different from that which one could imagine or expect. In the history of Christianity, the word faith has been reflected on from two different cultural backgrounds that merged. The first background is the Hebrew one, according to which believing is understood as similar to trusting. The second one is the Greek background that defines believing in relation to uncertain knowledge. Both elements play a role when we reflect on a religious perspective, and they are connected to each other in a circular way.

In order to trust God, we have to know whom we should trust. But this knowledge cannot be proved by any other knowledge than the knowledge acquired through trust. For this reason, the religious perspective can be supported by metaphors and analogies, but the experience of believing cannot be communicated fully. The insider's perspective differs radically from the outsider's perspective.

The difference between the two is similar to the theoretical knowledge about dying and the existential knowledge about one's own mortality we discussed in the first chapter.

We have chosen to understand the religious perspective as a relationship with God as the personal mystery of love. Living in this relationship one learns to see more with the eyes of the loved one (knowledge) and one's trust is developed as this way of life is experienced as valuable. What does this mean for the three meanings of death we discussed in Chapter 8?

In the light of faith, the face of death as a natural end of life is modified into death as the end of life on earth. In the Christian tradition life on earth is seen as a temporary existence during which one can develop a relationship with God. This relationship is called one's inner life, a life of grace, and this is seen as far more important than the life of the body. This spiritual core of a human being is preserved in and by God. The end of life on earth is the end of one's free development into a child of God. After death, God takes over.

The face of death as destroyer of bonds is also changed. On the one hand, it remains identical in that the grief and sorrow of being cut off from all the people one is connected to remains great. After death no more communication is possible. On the other hand, because all relationships are rooted in the central personal relationship with God, there can still be a connectedness between the living and the dying through God. Every Sunday the names of the departed are remembered and prayers are said. The church is a community of the living and the dead, because God is bigger than life and death.

Does this mean that the face of death as a door to the great unknown is changed? Again: yes and no. For Christians, death still remains a great mystery, a curtain behind which no one can look. Christians believe in a new stage behind that curtain, but this belief is a form of trust and confidence without any evidence or proof. In the Christian tradition many images have been developed going back to biblical sources and expressing in different ways in what direction one may hope.

The image of the Second Coming of Christ is a way of expressing that at the end of time, it is still this unique person who lived two thousand years ago in Galilee who will be the measure of humaneness. He will be the one who holds the Last Judgement – an image of God having the final judgement about our lives. The people who used their freedom in order to develop their love of God and do good will be rewarded, those who used their freedom in order to focus on their own interests solely will be punished. And again here, the central thought is that connectedness with God is the most important element.

Those who are connected with God will be given a new body in which this connectedness is expressed. There will be no more suffering, but complete harmony and happiness. This is the essence of heaven. Those who turn against God, turn against their own happiness. The idea of hell is nothing other than the expression of what it means when someone resists becoming the kind of person that God wants and invites us to be. Hell is the ultimate consequence of God's respect for human freedom, the freedom to refuse God.

The religious answer to the question: 'What can I hope for?' can be summarized in one sentence: to be safe in the loving hands of God. He knows what is best for us and he will take care of us after we have laid down our life on earth.

Limits and possibilities

Having worked out how the *ars moriendi* model works in a Christian mode, we have only observed one possibility among many others. Every religious tradition, path or philosophy of life will have its own way of reinterpreting the model according to its own needs and possibilities. The value of a shared *ars moriendi* might be that it functions as an interface that is helpful in understanding how different traditions can be related to a shared anthropological basis.

Having said that, I can think of at least two serious objections to this proposal. In the first place, one may argue that positioning the new *ars moriendi* as a quasi-neutral centre to which a variety of religions and philosophies of life can connect is in fact promoting a Christian model as the most central and important one: it is not surprising that in this chapter the model was easily reframed in Christian terms. Although it is true that the new *ars moriendi* is based on a medieval model of Christian origin, I hope that my deconstruction of the model in Chapter 2 into abstract and universal anthropological categories was thorough enough to convince the reader that I really have been looking for a universal anthropological framework open to as many different cultural contexts as possible.

In the second place, one might argue that my enterprise departs from the naive presupposition that there is something like an escape from the inherently Christian world view typical of North Atlantic culture. To this objection I can only say that I fully agree that universality and neutrality are highly problematic concepts, which are as much determined by the culture they are developed in as any other attempt to bridge gaps between languages and cultures. The new *ars moriendi* model was not developed as a theoretical framework for bringing world views together, but has been designed as a tool for the people who are confronted with the end of life in real life. In that sense, it is no less Christian and North Atlantic as the philosophy of palliative care itself.

This having been said, we will now turn to the last chapter where we will focus on the question of how the new *ars moriendi* model can be used in practice.

10

Working with the
Ars Moriendi Model

Mrs Balmes was 58 years old when she was admitted to the internal medicine ward. She was unable to eat or drink as a result of inoperable metastatic gastric carcinoma. The oncologist, a lady in her early sixties, had known Mrs Balmes since her gastric cancer diagnosis three years ago. Following chemotherapy and an operation during which her stomach had been removed, in the last two years there had seemed to be hope for survival. But the cancer had spread through her body again, and she had been treated with experimental chemotherapy. As this did not have any result, a laser treatment was started in order to improve her ability to eat and drink. Despite her treatment everything she swallowed came back. She was sitting in her bed with a bucket. Fluids were administered by intravenous therapy.

I heard about Mrs Balmes when the oncologist contacted me. Her relationship with this patient had always been a good one. She described her as a sweet woman, a mother of seven children, who had always worked hard for her family. Her husband was a local official who held a high position at the city administration and was often abroad.

Mrs Balmes was an active member of a very conservative Protestant denomination. She read the Bible on a daily basis, visited church twice every Sunday. There was no television in the house, and her children had never been vaccinated. Once in the hospital she was visited every day by an elder who read the Bible with her. During the day she was often seen with the book in her hands.

The administration of fluids had been started on her request, and she had also urged for administration of nutrition in order to live as long as possible. Her husband also asked that everything possible was done to prolong his wife's life.

In the last two days the oncologist had seen the woman crying every time she passed by. She seemed anxious. As she sat down to ask the woman what her greatest fear was, she said that she was afraid to die, or rather that she was sure that she was a sinful person and would burn in hell eternally. She hardly dared to go to sleep at night because she feared she would not wake up again.

In addition to this, she said she would love to speak to her eldest daughter. The girl had left home at the age of 18, because she had turned away from the church. She had got pregnant unexpectedly and had married the father of the child. They had two children, now aged 14 and 18 years old. Mrs Balmes's husband had refused any contact with her eldest daughter and also prohibited his wife from getting in touch with her. From time to time, however, the eldest daughter called her mother when Mrs Balmes's husband was abroad, but Mrs Balmes had never seen her grandchildren.

What does one do in a situation like this? What perspective does the new *ars moriendi* offer here and how could it support the difficult situation this 58-year-old woman was in? In this last chapter we will explore this case in order to see how the five questions of the new *ars moriendi* interrelate and how one can work with the *ars moriendi* model in practice.

Creating a culture of inner space

When I discuss this case during workshops, my first question is always about what hearing a case like this does to one's own inner space. As people start to report what they experience when hearing about this case, usually a great variety of emotions are described: anger towards the church that upholds a belief system that causes so much stress at the end of life; compassion or pity for the woman; an urge to put the woman in contact with her daughter and grandchildren before it is too late; resentment towards the husband who forbids his wife to be a good mother; recognition of this situation because it is precisely what happened to one's own grandmother; and many other reactions.

There are three reasons why it is important to start by exploring one's own inner space when working with the *ars moriendi* model. The first reason is because strong emotions are immediately felt by the patient and family. Strong feelings of indignation, anger or pity could work out in completely the wrong way in a case like this. One might think that Mrs Balmes might understand these emotions as an expression of empathy and solidarity with her situation, but it might well be that she interprets this reaction as a rejection of everything that is dear to her. The church and the loving attention of her husband have supported her all her life and still matter to her.

The second reason why it is important to start with exploring one's own inner space is because these strong impulses might also prevent an open-minded approach to the situation. One's emotions are triggered by one's own experiences and life history. When one hears a story, it is immediately interpreted and reframed through one's own experiences. How this works may be explained by an interesting experiment that stems from a hermeneutical approach to moral case deliberation where the participants are invited to invent a title for the case that in their view expresses what is at stake (Steinkamp and Gordijn 2003). With regard to Mrs Balmes, people come up with titles as diverse as 'longing mother and grandmother', 'how religion increases fear of death', and 'the trap of medical technology'. Every title frames the case in a different way, and limits the ways of looking at what could be done.

The third reason why we should start with exploring our inner space is because we are only able to attune to what Mrs Balmes needs if we are able to hear both our own inner voices and the questions behind her questions. Think about the example of Marie de Hennezel that we discussed in Chapter 3. Only by hearing our inner polyphony we can begin to reflect on how we should respond in the best possible way. If we want to help Mrs Balmes to develop inner space to deal with her situation, we must bring inner space with us ourselves and offer her a broader space to listen to what she experiences.

Approaching Mrs Balmes with inner space one can start to listen to her. During the actual conversation the *ars moriendi* model can play a role in different ways, depending on what fits best in the situation. We will first use the *ars moriendi* model as a framework for understanding Mrs Balmes's situation and detect where there is room to develop inner space, then we will discuss different ways in which the *ars moriendi* model can be used in practice. What follows, therefore, is an analysis that is separated from the actual dynamism of a conversation. For the sake of understanding how the five polarities work, however, it might be helpful to proceed this way.

The five polarities and their interrelation

The first question of the new *ars moriendi* is: 'Who am I and what do I really want?' We reflected on identity and autonomy within the polarity of me and the others. If we look at Mrs Balmes from this perspective, at first sight we see a woman whose identity is defined by many others. She has many roles in her life that connect her with other people. She is a spouse of a highly respected community officer, a mother of seven children, a member of a church, a child of God, and in all these roles it is clear what is expected of her and how she is supposed to behave.

What we do not know, and what is important to explore in a conversation, is to what extent she is also connected with herself in playing these roles. Connected with this is the question of the extent to which she is able to play these roles with inner space. We can catch a glimpse of her inner polyphony and the way roles are in conflict by the fact that she secretly has contact with her daughter although her husband has forbidden this.

One might think that the many roles she plays have restricted her freedom – being obedient to her husband, the church, God – but more important is the question of whether this obedience is combined with inner space and a connectedness with her me-pole. Moreover, the same structures and relations that have limited her freedom have also given her stability and security in life. They have been a framework that has helped her shape her life in a meaningful way.

The answer to the first question, and the freedom and inner space found there, is of great importance for the answer to the second question: 'How do I deal with suffering?' We reflected on this question within the polarity of doing and undergoing. Looking at the situation of Mrs Balmes from this perspective, we see that there is a great disparity between the physical dimension of care and the psychosocial and spiritual dimensions.

As for the physical part, we see that there is a lot of action-oriented activity: both she and her husband ask for everything to be done in order to keep her alive. And although she cannot eat or drink, and has no perspective of recovering, they want to keep her body going, even when this means that her suffering is prolonged. However, there seems to be little activity in the other three dimensions of palliative care. Mrs Balmes is afraid (psychological), she is cut off from her eldest daughter and her grandchildren (social), and afraid to burn in hell (spiritual).

The great disparity between these dimensions of care raises questions. A central question is why she and her husband want to do everything to prolong her living. The key to this may appear when we look at the interrelation between the different dimensions of care. One reason why she wants everything possible done to keep her alive might be that every day she lives longer will not be a day burning in hell. At the same time, every day she lives longer might be the day on which she could for the first time hold her grandchildren in her arms and say goodbye to her eldest daughter.

But there may be more reasons why there is so much emphasis on prolonging her life, that only become clear when one knows a bit more of the religious tradition she is part of. In orthodox traditions in Judaism, Christianity and Islam, there is a strong belief that

life is a gift of God, and only God is entitled to take it
back. It is therefore forbidden to do anything that may
hasten death or even increase the risk that life might be
shortened. Stopping with fluids and nutrition is often seen
as such an act, although in terminal patients it often only
increases suffering.

Next to the sanctity of life, a last religious motive for
prolongation of life might be the hope for acceptance
by God. According to the tradition to which Mrs
Balmes belongs, God chooses very few people to be united
with him in heaven. Most of the people who are born will
burn in hell. The few people who are chosen will know
this by a spiritual experience that cannot be forced, but
only hoped for by living a way of life that pleases God.
One is, however, not accepted by God because one has
led a morally perfect life, because this would compromise
God's sovereign freedom. The only reason why God
would accept a woman like Mrs Balmes is because this
is something that God wants. Every day that Mrs Balmes
lives longer is another day on which she may hope to
be accepted.

Looking at the polarity of doing and undergoing at first
sight there seems to be little inner space in Mrs Balmes.
But considering the many motives that keep her wanting
to stay alive, one discovers an inner force, a spirituality
that makes her cling to life, despite the suffering that it
brings. The question: 'How do I deal with suffering?' has
a very clear answer in her case. Suffering is part of the
process of dying. Also here her religious tradition may
play a role, as we will see in the polarity dealing with guilt.

The third question of the new *ars moriendi* is: 'How
can I say goodbye?' Within the polarity of holding on and
letting go, Mrs Balmes is clearly holding on to everything
she is connected to in life. She holds on to her physical

life, to what her husband and the church ask of her, to her children and grandchildren, and there seems to be no sign of letting go in any of these cases. Again the question is how much inner space she possesses in this area, because holding on may have the character of being freely connected with something that is very dear, or it may be a way of desperately clinging to something.

Considering that Mrs Balmes is a mother of seven children, it is striking that she only speaks about one daughter – the one who has left the house and is no longer a visible member of the family. For Mrs Balmes this is a great source of sorrow and the loss occupies her inner space. There seems to be a deep longing to see her daughter and grandchildren, and considering that palliative care focuses on both patient and relatives, one should say that it might be of great interest for both parties to investigate whether such an encounter could be organized: for Mrs Balmes in order to be able to let go of life, and for the others in order to have the consolation of saying goodbye.

As Mrs Balmes has lived with a secret connection with her daughter for many years, this might be the last chance to reconcile. However, this can hardly be done without involving the other family members. Her husband of course plays a central role here, but also her six other children might be a valuable resource for building a bridge between the husband and the daughter. As Mrs Balmes is at the centre of her family, her death will have great impact on her husband, children and grandchildren. Mourning is a social practice.

Mrs Balmes might only be able to let go of life when she has held her daughter and grandchildren. But even if this is not possible, there might be a way of helping Mrs Balmes to hold on to her daughter and grandchildren in a different way, with more inner space. For example, she might write or dictate a letter to them in order to express her feelings and say goodbye to them. Or she may hold on to them in her prayers.

The fourth question of the *ars moriendi* is: 'How do I look back on my life?' Mrs Balmes is a religious woman and in her view the question of how she looks back on her life is less important than the question of how God judges her. From that perspective she might have a number of worries concerning the guilt that she has on her shoulders. In her tradition, the majority of human beings are doomed and only a small minority is saved. The reason for being doomed from the outset is not because of one's own actual sins, but because the human race were doomed once Adam and Eve were insubordinate to God. From this moment on, human beings have been defective and not able to do good. This is the reason why she will burn in hell.

On top of this, there are a number of other things that may make her feel guilty, and which are all related to the most important relationships in her life: she has failed in educating her eldest daughter well; she has kept secrets from her husband; she has transgressed the rules of God and the church; she has not fought to keep her daughter in the family; she has not fought to see her grandchildren.

Looking back on her life, it seems that Mrs Balmes is rather stuck to the pole of remembering, with not much inner space to create new perspectives on her situation. It might be the case that we will have to talk to her husband – to whom she keeps holding on – in order to create inner space. What have been the motives for sending his daughter away? Has it been the love for his other children, to protect them from negative influences? Has it been shame about his failure to educate his daughter correctly? Has it been pressure from his social environment and fear of losing face? Has it been anger and frustration at not being able to reach his daughter? There might be a multitude of motives – an inner polyphony – by which this decision has been made. Bringing them to light may help to him to reconsider if perhaps his daughter has been punished enough by now, and whether his wife's situation merits an attitude of mercifulness and reconciliation. In the end, helping Mr Balmes to create inner space inside himself is important to both himself, Mrs Balmes and the entire family.

In the process of speaking with Mr Balmes, inner space is also a quality that is required by the caregivers: if he clings to the pole of remembering as well, and is unable to admit perspectives other than his own, it is important to respect him for his feelings.

The fifth question of the new *ars moriendi* is: 'What can I hope for?' As we have seen that Mrs Balmes has a great fear of dying because of the fear of burning in hell, the answer to this question seems to be clear. In the polarity between knowing and believing she seems to be clinging to the position that we have described as fideism. There is only one external authority, the Bible as interpreted by her tradition, and this authority is clear about her future perspective.

Working towards creating inner space in this field is difficult, but the same sovereignty of God that forbids any speculation about being chosen or not, may also remain a source of hope. And religiously speaking, the thought that only God knows what is best for me or what I deserve, may be a stepping stone towards a more accepting attitude towards what will happen in the future. An alternative way of working towards inner space may be to read the Bible with her. Allowing the inner polyphony of Mrs Balmes to resonate with the polyphony of her tradition may divert her attention from the fear of hell towards sources helping her to bear the burden that God puts on our shoulders.

Having discussed all five questions of the new *ars moriendi*, we have seen that every question offers a different perspective to the complex situation of Mrs Balmes. Every question can also be an opening to help the woman and her family develop more inner space in order to bear their situation and work towards a good death. How this process will develop is dependent on many factors, among which the inner space of those involved plays a major role. And as we have seen, all five questions are different entries to the same complex situation of Mrs Balmes.

Five ways of putting the *ars moriendi* model into practice

In this final section we will discuss five ways in which the *ars moriendi* model may be helpful at the end of life. These five ways were developed in different practices in the Netherlands and Belgium during the last twelve years. They may give an impression of the many possibilities that are offered by the *ars moriendi* model. But they may also be seen as an invitation to develop new ways of working with the model.

The new *ars moriendi* is designed as a framework for dealing with the big questions at the end of life. Strictly speaking, *ars moriendi* is the art of the one who is dying: this is reflected in the five central questions of the model, which are personal questions for each of us. But since dying in our culture is framed in a variety of healthcare practices, and since human beings are social beings, we will approach the *ars moriendi* here as a social practice in which the dying, in dialogue with relatives, formal and informal caregivers, prepare us for the final farewell. The perspective chosen here is sometimes that of the patient and sometimes that of the caregiver, or a combination of the two.

A first way of working with the model – being a patient, a relative or a caregiver – is to use it as a mirror for ourselves. It confronts us with the question of how much inner space we have, and helps us to discover and give room to the polyphony inside us. It also may help in realizing that all people involved live with this inner polyphony. Sometimes one aspect resonates very strongly with someone in some ways, while feeling completely different in other ways. For patients, understanding and accepting that in the dying process one is sometimes torn between different positions inside oneself can help to develop inner freedom. For caregivers, in order to be able to meet the spiritual needs of patients, it is important that they are able to demonstrate the reflective capacity to consider the importance of spiritual and existential dimensions in their own lives (Gamondi, Larkin and Payne 2013a, 2013b).

Working with the *ars moriendi* model requires some reflective capacities and the ability to be both critical of and compassionate towards oneself. For those who have these capacities, the model is not only helpful at the end of life. Reflecting on the human condition one will discover that the five polarities are like universal anthropological themes that are relevant throughout our lives. For those who lack these capacities, it may be more helpful to use the model in one of the other ways that will be described and that are more interactive.

A second way of working with the model is using it as a tool to open up a conversation. In the Rijnstate Hospital in Arnhem, the Netherlands, for example, the palliative care nurse offers patients a leaflet with a graphical version of the model in order to help them organize their thoughts (Voskuilen 2012). Patients take these leaflets home, and in a follow-up conversation they are free to talk about what has come up looking at the model. The experience reported by the nurses is that the model covers all possible existential issues that are raised, although some patients have difficulty understanding concepts like autonomy. The most important contribution to their process is that the model helps them to organize their thoughts. Unique in this way of caring is the fact that patients are offered a hold to get a grip on their existential questions themselves. And they can take the lead in deciding how they want to share these questions with their caregivers.

A third way of working with the model is to use it as a mirror for our own conversations on the spiritual dimension at the end of life. Conversations on spiritual issues are often held in a free way – usually the caregiver attunes to the conversation partner and the conversation unfolds in a more or less dialogical and intuitive way. Although this has great merits, it may lead to a certain one-sidedness. During a spiritual care education session for physicians and chaplains it was striking that professionals from both groups easily embarked on a conversation on the first three questions of the *ars moriendi* model but consciously or subconsciously avoided talking about the fourth and the fifth questions (Leget, van Daelen and Swart 2013). Guilt, shame and faith are considered to be private and intimate matters, not easily talked about. By making notes about the conversation afterwards and organizing one's reflections within the bipolar framework of the *ars moriendi* model, one may discover which issues one prefers to talk about and which themes are not discussed. The more one works in this way, the more the model will begin to function as a framework for understanding and organizing one's thoughts during the conversation. When this becomes a habit, the conversation may become free and provide a framework for critical self-reflection.

This brings us to a fourth way of using the model: as a tool for communicating, reporting and interpreting the concerns of patients and families (Leget *et al.* 2008). In a context where people do not talk easily about their spiritual concerns, collecting and organizing the fragments in the framework of the *ars moriendi* model has two advantages. In the first place, this dimension of care becomes visible in the system and gives support for those who are in need of a concrete model in order to be able to report spiritual issues. This model is especially helpful because it integrates many medical ethical issues concerning autonomy, treatment decisions and advanced care planning with the spiritual dimension. In the second place, such a shared framework helps develop a shared language and frame of reference for talking about this dimension of palliative care and its importance for total care.

Although in some countries chaplains are reluctant to share confidential information about the spiritual issues of patients – and confidentiality is indeed an important condition for good spiritual care – the new *ars moriendi* model can be used to communicate the areas where issues important to other disciplines can be located, without breaking the rules of confidentiality.

In a fifth way, the *ars moriendi* model can be used for education about spiritual and ethical issues. One of the problems in the education of spiritual care is that the subject appears to be vague or abstract to many people. Many times this leads to irritation or rejection of the subject of spirituality. The big questions of life seem to be too overwhelming and hard to grasp. By presenting the *ars moriendi* model the caregivers – just as the patients in the first way of working with the model – are offered a concrete map of the field that helps them to organize their thoughts. The diamond-shaped model that is found at the end of Chapter 2 can be used as such a map.

Regarding the diamond shape of the model, two reflections can be helpful. First, the fact that inner space is at the centre immediately makes clear that inner space is what the new *ars moriendi* is all about. As we have seen throughout this book, inner space helps in dealing with inner polyphony, understanding different positions and improving the quality of the dying process. Inner space is at the beginning and the end of the new *ars moriendi* as a precondition and foundation, and as a quality indicator and aim.

Second, the five sides of the model are like the facets of a diamond: every facet casts new light on a situation and offers a new perspective. It is of little importance in what order the five polarities are explored; the point is to what degree they cast light on the existential struggles of people and offer a framework for discovering inner space. To what extent this is successful is not just dependent on the *ars moriendi* model – it is the people working with the model who can make it shine.

References

Ariès, P. (1991) *The Hour of Our Death.* Oxford: University Press.

Bauman, Z. (2000) *Liquid Modernity.* Cambridge: Polity Press.

Bayard, F. (1999) *L'art du bien mourir au XVe siècle.* Paris: Presses de l'Université Paris-Sorbonne.

Beauvoir, S. de (1964) *Une mort très douce.* Paris: Gallimard.

Becker, E. (1973) *The Denial of Death.* New York: Simon and Schuster.

Bout, J. van den (1999) 'Het ongewone van "gewone" rouw.' In J. van den Bout, P. Poelen, R. Bruntink, J. Enklaar and M. Klaassen (eds) *Handboek sterven, uitvaart, en rouw.* Maarssen: Elsevier, IV 1.1–20.

Brown, W. (2003) 'Neoliberalism and the end of liberal democracy.' *Theory & Event* 7:1 (no page).

Brugère, F. (2014) 'Care and its political effects.' In G. Olthuis, H. Kohlen and J. Heier (eds) *Moral Boundaries Redrawn. The Significance of Joan's Tronto Argument for Political Theory, Professional Ethics, and Care as a Practice.* Leuven: Peeters.

Callahan, D. (1988) *Setting Limits. Medical Goals in an Aging Society.* New York: Simon and Schuster.

Cassell, E. (2004) *The Nature of Suffering and the Goals of Medicine.* Oxford: Oxford University Press.

Chochinov, H. (2002) 'Dignity-conserving care – a new model for palliative care: helping the patient feel valued.' *Journal of the American Medical Association 287*, 2253–2260.

Chochinov, H. *et al.* (2005) 'Dignity therapy: a novel psychotherapeutic intervention for patients near the end of life.' *Journal of Clinical Oncology 23*, 5520–5525.

Collett, L. and Lester, D. (1969) 'The fear of death and dying.' *Journal of Psychology 72*, 179–81.

Dastur, F. (1995) *La mort: essay sur la finitude.* Paris: Hatier.

Dixon, T. (2003) *From Passions to Emotions: The Creation of a Secular Psychological Category.* Cambridge: Cambridge University Press.

Dubet, F. (2002) *Le déclin de l'institution.* Paris: Seuil.

Elias, N. (1985) *The Loneliness of the Dying.* Oxford: Blackwell.

Frankl, V. (2006) *Man's Search for Meaning.* Boston, MA: Beacon Press.

Gamondi, C., Larkin, P. and Payne, S. (2013a) 'Core competencies in palliative care: an EAPC white paper on palliative care education: part 1.' *European Journal of Palliative Care 20*, 2, 86–91.

Gamondi, C., Larkin, P. and Payne, S. (2013b) 'Core competencies in palliative care: an EAPC white paper on palliative care education: part 2.' *European Journal of Palliative Care 20*, 3, 140–145.

Girard-Augry, P. (1986) *Ars moriendi (1492) ou L'art de bien mourir.* Paris: Dervy.

Gorer, G. (1965) 'The pornography of death.' Encounter 5. In G. Gorer (ed.) *Death, Grief and Mourning.* New York: Routledge.

Hansen, F. (2012) 'One step further: the dance between poetic dwelling and socratic wonder in phenomenological research. *Indo-Pacific Journal of Phenomenology 12*, (Special edition), 1–2.

Hennezel, M. de (1998) *La Mort intime.* Paris: Robert Laffont.

Hennezel, M. de (2000) *Nous ne nous sommes pas dit au revoir. La dimension humaine du débat sur l'euthanasie.* Paris: Robert Laffont.

Heijst, A. van (2011) *Professional Loving Care.* Leuven: Peeters.

Jankélévich, V. (1966) *La Mort.* Paris: Flammarion.

John Paul II, Pope (1984) *Salvifici doloris: Apostolic letter of His Holiness John Paul II on the Christian meaning of human suffering.* Boston: Daughters of St. Paul.

Kellehear, A. (2016) 'The nature of contemporary dying: obsessions, distortions, challenges.' *Studies in Christian Ethics 29*, 245–248.

Kennedy, J. (2002) *Een weloverwogen dood. Euthanasie in Nederland.* Amsterdam: Bert Bakker.

Kirchhoffer, D. (2013) *Human Dignity in Contemporary Ethics.* Amherst, NY: Teneo Press.

Klass, D., Silverman, P.R. and Nickman, S.L. (1996) *Continuing Bonds: New Understandings of Grief.* Philadelphia: Taylor & Francis.

Kübler-Ross, E. (1969) *On Death and Dying.* New York: The Macmillan Company.

Kylmä, J. and Vehviläinen-Julkunen, K. (1997) 'Hope in nursing research: a meta-analysis of the ontological and epistemological foundations of research on hope.' *Journal of Advanced Nursing 25*, 2, 364–71.

Laager, J. (1996) *Ars moriendi. Die Kunst gut zu leben und gut zu sterben: Texte von Cicero bis Luther.* Zurich: Manesse Verlag.

Larochefoucauld, F. (2002) *Réflexions ou sentences et maximes morales et réflexions diverses.* Laurence Plazenet (ed.) Paris, Champion.

Lawton, J. (1998) 'Contemporary hospice care: the sequestration of the unbounded body and "dirty dying".' *Sociology of Health & Illness 20*, 2, 121–143.

Lawton, J. (2000) *The Dying Process. Patients' Experiences of Palliative Care.* London and New York: Routledge.

Leget, C. (1997) *Living with God: Thomas Aquinas on the Relation between Life on Earth and 'Life' after Death.* Leuven: Peeters.

Leget, C. (2000) 'Moral theology upside down. Aquinas' treatise *de passionibus animae* considered through the lens of its spatial metaphors.' *Yearbook 1999 of the Thomas Institute at Utrecht.* Utrecht: Thomas Insitute.

Leget, C. (2003) *Ruimte om te sterven. Een weg voor zieken, naasten en zorgverleners.* Tielt: Lannoo.

Leget, C. (2008) *Van levenskunst tot stervenskunst. Over spiritualiteit in de palliatieve zorg.* Tielt: Lannoo.

Leget, C. (2013a) 'Assisted dying – the current debate in the Netherlands.' *European Journal of Palliative Care 20*, 4, 168–171.

Leget, C. (2013b) 'Analyzing dignity: a perspective from the ethics of care.' *Medicine, Health Care and Philosophy 16*, 945–52.

Leget, C., Daelen, M. van and Swart, S. (2013) 'Spirituele zorg in de kaderopleiding Palliatieve Zorg.' *Tijdschrift voor Ouderengeneeskunde 3*, 146–149.

Leget, C., Rubbens, L., Lissnijder, L. and Menten, J. (2008) 'Naar een spirituele "checklist" in een palliatieve zorgeenheid.' *Nederlands Tijdschrift voor Palliatieve Zorg 8*, 3, 93–101.

Lommel, P. van, Wees, R. van, Meyers, V. and Elfferich, I. (2001) 'Near-death experience in survivors of cardiac arrest: a prospective study in the Netherlands.' *Lancet 358*, 9298, 2039–2045.

Mahoney, J. (1987) *The Making of Moral Theology: A Study of the Roman Catholic Tradition.* Oxford: University Press.

Manschot, H. (2003) 'De betekenis van het tragische voor de ethiek van zorg – en hulpverlening.' In H. Manschot and H. van Dartel (eds) *In gesprek over goede zorg. Overlegmethoden voor ethiek in de praktijk.* Amsterdam: Boom.

Merleau-Ponty, M. (1945) *Phénoménologie de la perception.* Paris: Gallimard.

Nussbaum, M. (1986) *The Fragility of Goodness. Luck and Ethics in Greek Tragedy and Philosophy.* Cambridge: Cambridge University Press.

Nussbaum, M. (2001) *Upheavals of Thought. The Intelligence of Emotions.* Cambridge: Cambridge University Press.

Olsman, E., Leget, C., Onwuteaka-Philipsen, B. and Willems, D. (2014) 'Should palliative care patients' hope be truthful, helpful or valuable? An interpretative synthesis of literature describing healthcare professionals' perspectives on hope of palliative care patients.' *Palliative Medicine 28*, 1, 59–70.

Olsman, E., Leget, C., Duggleby, W. and Willems, D. (2015) 'A singing choir: understanding the dynamics of hope, hopelessness, and despair in palliative care patients. A longitudinal qualitative study.' *Palliative and Supportive Care 13*, 6, 1643–1650.

Oz, A. (2010) *How to Cure a Fanatic.* Princeton: Princeton University Press.

Puchalski, C., Ferrell, B., Virani, R., Otis-Green, S., Baird, P., Bull, J. and Pugliese, K. (2009). 'Improving the quality of spiritual care as a dimension of palliative care: The report of the Consensus Conference.' *Journal of Palliative Medicine, 12*, 10, 885–904.

Puchalski, C. M., Vitillo, R., Hull, S. K. and Reller, N. (2014). 'Improving the spiritual dimension of whole person care: Reaching national and international consensus.' *Journal of Palliative Medicine, 17*, 6, 642–656.

Ricoeur, P. (1990) *Soi-même comme un autre.* Paris: Seuil.

Scarry, E. (1985) *The Body in Pain: the Making and Unmaking of the World.* Oxford: University Press.

Scherer, K.R. (2005) 'What are emotions and how can they be measured?' *Social Science Information 44*, 4, 695–729.

Schotsmans, P. and Meulenbergs, T. (2005) *Euthanasia and Palliative Care in the Low Countries*. Leuven: Peeters.

Seale, C. (1998) *Constructing Death. The Sociology of Dying and Bereavement*. Cambridge: Cambridge University Press.

Seymour, J.E. (2000) 'Negotiating natural death in intensive care.' *Social Science & Medicine 51*, 8, 1241–1252.

Simpson, M.A. (1979) *Dying, Death and Grief: A Critical Bibliography*. Philadelphia: University of Philadelphia Press.

Smeele, H. (2002) *Met de moed van een ontdekkingsreiziger*. Utrecht: Servire.

Sokolowski, R. (1982) *The God of Faith and Reason: Foundations of Christian Theology*. Notre Dame and London: University of Notre Dame Press.

Stamperius, H. (2009) Hannes Meinkema, interview by Iris Pronk in newspaper *Trouw*. Accessible at www.trouw.nl/tr/nl/4324/Nieuws/article/detail/1172192/2009/10/17/Hannes-Meinkema.dhtml, accessed on 23 July 2016.

Steinkamp, N. and Gordijn, B. (2003) 'Ethical case deliberation on the ward. A comparison of four methods.' *Medicine, Health Care and Philosophy 6*, 3, 235–246.

Stroebe, M. and Schut, H. (1999) 'The dual process model of coping with bereavement: Rationale and description.' *Death Studies 23*, 3, 197–224.

Süsskind, P. (1985) *Das Parfüm: Die Geschichte eines Mörders*. Diogenes: Zurich.

Taylor, C. (1985) *Philosophical Papers*. Cambridge: Cambridge University Press.

Taylor, C. (1991) *The Ethics of Authenticity*. Cambridge, MA and London: Harvard University Press.

Thich Nhat Hanh (1975) *The Miracle of Mindfulness*. New York: Beacon Press.

Tillich, P. (1952) *The Courage To Be*. New Haven: Yale University Press.

Tongeren, P. van (2003) *Deugdelijk leven. Een inleiding in de deugdethiek*. Nijmegen: SUN.

Tronto, J. (1993) *Moral Boundaries: A Political Argument for an Ethic of Care*. New York and London: Routledge.

Voskuilen, J. (2012) *Levensvragen van patiënten en het Ars moriendi model: Een kwalitatief onderzoek naar de betekenis die palliatieve patiënten geven aan de thema's van het Ars moriendi model*. Thesis: Hogeschool Arnhem Nijmegen, Master of Advanced Nursing.

Walker, M. (2007) *Moral Understandings: A Feminist Study in Ethics*, 2nd revised edition. Oxford: Oxford University Press.

Walter, T. (1994) *The Revival of Death*. London: Routledge.

Wijngaarden, E.J. van, Leget, C.J.W. and Goossensen, A. (2016) 'Disconnectedness from the here-and-now: A phenomenological perspective as a counteract on the medicalisation of death wishes in elderly people.' *Medicine, Healthcare and Philosophy 19*, 2, 265–73.

Worden, J.W. (2002) *Grief Counseling and Grief Therapy: A Handbook for the Mental Health Practitioner*. New York: Springer Publishing Company.

Subject Index

action *see* doing
afterlife, rationality and 159–60
agnosticism 160
anxiety
  three types of 24–5
  versus fear 24
Aquinas, Thomas 15, 17, 72–3, 102,
  106, 181
architectural environment 68
Aristotle 21, 71–2
ars moriendi medieval model
  block prints of 40, 44–6
  five temptations in 40–3
  limitations for modern use 43–4
  moralistic approach of 50–1
  overview of 39–43
  translated into twenty-first century
    language 45
ars moriendi model
  case study 191–201
  diamond shaped model 57, 205
  for education about spiritual and
    ethical issues 204–5
  five struggles reframed in 53–7
  guidelines/protocols and 73–4
  inner space at centre of 49–53
  'moral understandings' and 52
  overview of 44
  in practice 201–5
  reinterpretation of medieval tradition
    and 44–6
  as tool for communicating 202–4

ars vivendi 38–9
assisted dying
  and culture of self-determination 81
  debates around introduction of 16
  physician-patient interaction
    regarding 47–8
  secular dogmatism about 16
autonomy *see* self
avarice
  in *ars moriendi* contemporary model
    54–5
  in *ars moriendi* medieval model 41–2

'Black Death' 39–40
body
  non-verbal bodily expressions 68
  object body 32, 111–2
  as road to inner space 66–8
  subject body 32, 111–2
  transgression of boundaries of 34
body-mind dualism 32

chaplaincy, outcome-oriented 12–3
charity
  in *ars moriendi* contemporary model
    54–5
  in *ars moriendi* medieval model 42
choice, increasing complexity of
  99–100
Collett-Lester Fear of Death Scale 23
communities, imagined 28–9

Author Index